The highest recommendation I can give to this wonderful book is that I will be reading it over and over again to my children. It is rich in biblical doctrine and is an invaluable instrument to aid parents in teaching their children the glorious truths of "God in Christ" reconciling the world to Himself. I know of no other book that so clearly communicates the great doctrines of the gospel to children. I look forward to hearing of the harvest that it will reap in the years to come.

– Paul Washer,
Author, Director of HeartCry Missionary Society

Jennifer Adams has a present for your child, a gift of biblical truth, wrapped in love. Three features make this book especially valuable. First, it teaches children gospel truths about God, sin, Christ, and the gospel call in short and simple chapters. Second, each point is carefully referenced to Scripture. Third, it concludes with a valuable Bible study for your child to look up and write out the same truths found in each chapter. This is an excellent tool that God can use to bring your children to Jesus Christ to find salvation in Him alone.

– Dr. Joel R. Beeke,
President, Puritan Reformed Theological Seminary,
Grand Rapids, Michigan

THE
Gospel
MADE
CLEAR
to Children

THE
Gospel
MADE
CLEAR
to Children

JENNIFER ADAMS

ILLUSTRATED BY ELISABETH ADAMS

FREE GRACE PRESS

Published by
Free Grace Press
3900 Dave Ward Dr., Ste. 1900
Conway, AR 72034
(501) 214-9663
email: support@freegracepress.com
website: www.freegracepress.com

Printed in the United States of America

Cover design by Scott Schaller
Illustrations Copyright ©2022 Elisabeth Adams

ISBN: 978-1-952599-39-2

For additional Reformed Baptist titles, please email us for a free list or see our website at the above address.

To My Daughters

Mary Bethany
Elisabeth Victoria
Sarah Kate
Anna Grace

This book is for you, your children,
and your children's children.

Contents

Acknowledgments

I wrote this book for my daughters nine years ago. Since then, numerous people assisted with preparing it for publication. They read the manuscript, provided helpful feedback, and assisted with layout. Their contributions are significant, and I thank the Lord for them. Many thanks to my husband, Scott, for encouragement to write and the support of my theological pursuits.

Thank you to Anthony Mathenia for recommending the book for publication. Thank you to Elzeline Hite, Kirsten Keusal, and Melissa Madsen for prayer support and encouragement.

Thank you to Jeffrey Johnson, Liz Smith, and the wonderful staff at Free Grace Press for editing, typesetting, adding the glossary, and bringing the book to completion.

Special thanks to my daughter Mary for cheering me on throughout its production and to my daughter Elisabeth for her beautiful illustrations. Heartfelt thanks to my daughters Sarah Kate and Anna Grace for working through it with me several times.

Finally, thank you to Paul and Charo Washer for support, theological review, numerous suggestions, and permission to quote from Paul's sermons and books.

A Word to Parents

This book attempts to explain God's love to children as it is manifested in the gospel of Christ. It is written for parents to read aloud to younger children (elementary) and for older children (youth) to work through independently. Corresponding study questions can be found in the companion guide. Words in **bold** are found in the glossary. Footnotes have been provided to give parents additional information. It is our prayer that the Lord may use this book to help parents impart to their children the wisdom that leads to salvation (2 Timothy 3:15).

A Word to Children

Dear children, this book is written with a heart full of love for you. The greatest gift anyone can give is the knowledge of God and the salvation that is found in His Son, Jesus Christ. However, before you can receive this gift, there are some truths from God's Word you must hear. If you are willing to listen, these truths will lead to the greatest blessing imaginable.

Those who hear God's words and act on them are like the wise man who built his house on the rock. When the rains came and the winds blew and the floods burst against the house, it stood firm. But those who hear God's words and do not act on them are like the foolish man who built his house on the sand. When the rains came and the winds blew and the floods burst against the house, it fell, and great was its fall (Matthew 7:24–27).

Jesus gave us the above parable to warn us. It is not enough to hear God's Word. We must act on His Word by faith. We do not want to be like the foolish man who built his life on the sand and was destroyed, but like the wise man who built his life on the rock of God's Word and stood firm. Therefore, take a moment and pray. Ask God to help you understand His Word and act on it.

As a final note, if your parents have asked you to read this book, or if they are reading it to you, please know that they are doing this because they love you and care about you. Please honor them by your willingness to read, listen, and carefully consider the holiness of God, the sinful condition of your soul, and the provision God has made for you in His Son, Jesus Christ. This will bless them—and you—more than you know.

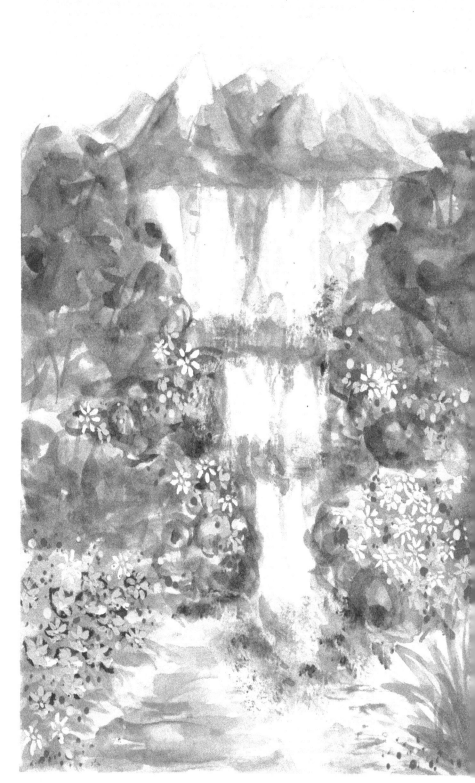

PART 1

God's Person and Worth

Holy, Holy, Holy, is the LORD of hosts,
The whole earth is full of His glory.

– Isaiah 6:3

1

High and Holy
God's Attributes and Worth

For thus says the high and exalted One
Who lives forever, whose name is Holy,
"I dwell on a high and holy place."

– Isaiah 57:15

ear children, there is no better place to begin than with the knowledge of God. We can know about God by studying His attributes. Do you know what an attribute is? An attribute tells us something about a person so we can know him or her. We might say Mary is loving and Elisabeth is sweet, or Sarah is fun and Anna is cute. Now you know something about my daughters. Can you think of some attributes that describe the people in your family?

Did you know that God has attributes too? The Bible tells us His attributes so we can know Him. The Bible says God is high and lifted up.[1] He is **exalted** over all creation because He is the Creator of all.[2] He is the sovereign Lord over everything![3] There is no place in heaven or on earth that can contain Him.[4] There is no part of creation that is not under His rule.[5] The kingdoms of this world are like a drop in a bucket compared to the power and scope of God's majesty and reign![6]

Although we cannot see God, the prophet Isaiah gives us a glimpse of His glory. Isaiah reveals that God is the center of heaven, where He is seated on the throne, receiving worship from angels and **saints**. Shouts of joy mingle with peals of thunder and songs of praise. The seraphim continually cry, "Holy, Holy, Holy, is the Lord of hosts. The whole earth is full of His glory" (Isaiah 6:3). Even though the seraphim have never sinned, they cover their faces because they are not worthy to look upon Him. They desire to behold His beauty but dare not draw near.

Before God's throne are mysterious "living creatures."[7] They are strange-looking and put fear in our hearts. They cry out, "Holy, holy, holy is the Lord God, the Almighty, who was and who is and who is to come" (Revelation 4:8). These creatures tell us that God is different from His creation. He does not compare with anything He has made.[8] There is no one like Him.[9]

While mysterious, high, and holy, God is good.[10] He is the fountain of all goodness. He is full of compassion and kindness. He cares for people by providing for their needs.[11] He blesses them with rain, sunshine, food, and gladness.[12] Every good gift comes from Him.[13]

God is powerful.[14] He has power to do all His holy will. His good plans always come about because He has all power to do them.[15] No one can ruin His plans. His good purposes always prevail.

God is sovereign.[16] He rules over all. Not even a bird falls to the ground without His knowing.[17] He appoints worms.[18] He commands fish.[19] He rebukes winds.[20] People make their plans, but God directs their steps.[21] People roll the dice, but God determines the outcome.[22] God has appointed a time and a season for every single event that happens.[23]

God is **just**.[24] He deals with all people by the same standard—His law.[25] He **renders** just judgments.[26] He deals righteously with everyone because He is righteous.[27] He always does right.[28]

God is wise.[29] He knows the best thing to do all the time. He is never confused or unsure. He is never mistaken or deceived. He cannot be fooled or tricked. He always has the right answer for everything! He has perfect understanding of how all things work.[30] He knows how to take what people mean for evil and work it for good![31] No problem is too difficult for Him. Even the most difficult question of all—how He can be just and **justify** sinners[32]—cannot stump Him. His wisdom makes people and angels speechless! They stand in awe of His ways.

Did you know there are some things God cannot do? God cannot sin because He is holy.[33] There is not an ounce of sin within Him. He never has a sinful thought or desire. He is perfectly pure.[34]

God cannot lie because He is truth.[35] There is no dishonesty with God.[36] He is not crafty or deceitful. He does not pretend or trick people. He does not mistreat or wrong them.

God is faithful because He cannot deny Himself.[37] He always deals with people based on His Word. He never breaks His Word. He keeps all His good promises—not one of them will fail.[38] He is a covenant-keeping God.[39]

God cannot change.[40] He has always been and always will be the same.[41] He is infinite in all His attributes—this means that His holiness, goodness, love, mercy, power, wisdom, faithfulness, righteousness, and justice go on and on and on without measure, forever![42] He will always be the same good, righteous, holy God!

God is beyond **comprehension**. People can only know what God chooses to reveal about Himself.[43] God has graciously chosen to reveal Himself through His Son.[44] We see His Son in the Scriptures. Even still, there is so much more to God than our limited minds can grasp. God's ways are beyond our ability to explain; they are higher than our ways because they are marvelous![45] He is worthy of worship!

Do you know where God is? God is everywhere.[46] He is in heaven, receiving worship from angels and saints.[47] He is on earth, preserving and governing people's lives.[48] He is in hell, giving unrepentant sinners and disobedient angels just payment for their sins.[49]

God knows all things.[50] He knows everything about you. He knows where you live, what you do, and what matters most to you. He knows the future because He planned it. He can be trusted with every detail of your life because He cares for you.[51]

God can see all things.[52] He sees what you are doing all the time, even when no one else is looking.[53] He knows the secrets of your heart.[54]

What else is God doing from His throne? Isaiah tells us He is redeeming sinners and making them holy. He is filling the earth with His glory.[55] He alone is worthy!

Notes

1   Isaiah 57:15

2   Isaiah 45:12; Revelation 4:11

3   Isaiah 6:1; Jeremiah 23:24; Isaiah 66:1

4   1 Kings 8:27

5   Psalm 103:19

6   Daniel 4:34–35; Isaiah 40:15, 17

7   Revelation 4:8

8   Isaiah 40:18

9   Isaiah 46:9; 1 Samuel 2:2

10   Psalm 136:1

11   Matthew 5:45

12   Acts 14:17

13   James 1:17

14   Psalm 62:11

15   Daniel 2:20

16   Psalm 103:19

17   Matthew 10:29

18   Jonah 4:7

19   Jonah 1:17

20   Mark 4:39–41

21   Proverbs 16:9

22   Proverbs 16:33

23   Ecclesiastes 3:1

24   Deuteronomy 32:4

25   James 2:10–12

26   Zephaniah 3:5

27   Genesis 18:25

28   Psalm 92:15

29   Romans 16:27

30   Psalm 147:5

31   Genesis 50:20

32   Romans 3:26

33   James 1:13; Isaiah 6:3; Psalm 77:13

34   1 John 3:3; Habakkuk 1:13; James 3:17

35   Numbers 23:19; John 14:6

36   James 1:17

37   Deuteronomy 7:9; 2 Timothy 2:13

38 Joshua 21:45; 2 Corinthians 1:20

39 Deuteronomy 7:9

40 Malachi 3:6

41 Hebrews 13:8; Psalm 102:26–27; Revelation 1:4

42 Psalm 147:5

43 Deuteronomy 29:29

44 Hebrews 1:2

45 Romans 11:33–34; Isaiah 40:28; Isaiah 55:8–9; Psalm 118:23

46 Psalm 139:7

47 Psalm 139:8; Revelation 4:2

48 Proverbs 15:3

49 Psalm 139:8; R.C. Sproul observes, "A breath of relief is usually heard when someone declares, 'Hell is a symbol for separation from God.' To be separated from God for eternity is no great threat to the impenitent person. The ungodly want nothing more than to be separated from God. Their problem in hell will not be separation from God; it will be the presence of God that will torment them. In hell, God will be present in the fullness of His divine wrath. He will be there to exercise His just punishment of the damned. They will know Him as an all-consuming fire." R.C. Sproul, "Hell," Bible Research, http://www.bible-researcher.com/hell6.html; see also R.C. Sproul, Essential Truths of the Christian Faith (Wheaton, Illinois: Tyndale House, 1992), 285–287.

50 1 John 3:20

51 I Peter 5:7; Matthew 5:25-26

52 Proverbs 15:3

53 Hebrews 4:13

54 Romans 2:16

2

Dwelling in Perfect Delight
The Father, Son, and Spirit

Baptizing them in the name of the Father
and the Son and the Holy Spirit.

– *Matthew 28:19*

ear children, do you know someone who is perfectly happy? If you answered "God," you are right! God is complete and happy in Himself.[1] He cannot be robbed of His happiness. He does not need anyone or anything.[2]

Do you ever wonder what God did before He made the world? He simply enjoyed Himself! He dwelt in perfect unity as Father, Son, and Spirit.

Do you know what a **mystery** is? It is something hidden. Only God can reveal mysteries about Himself. God's Word reveals a very special mystery—it says that He is one God in three persons—Father, Son, and Spirit.[3] The Father is God. The Son is God. The Spirit is God. They are three persons but one God. We call this mystery the Trinity. Before making the world, the Father and Son enjoyed sweet fellowship with one another by the Spirit.[4] Their happiness in one another is the highest happiness of all. The Father delights in the Son.[5] The Son delights in honoring the Father.[6] The Spirit glorifies both the Father and the Son.[7] The Father, Son, and Spirit take so much delight in one another that their happiness spills over into creation.[8] All true happiness known by God's people is a tiny drop of the ocean of God's happiness as the triune God.

The Father, Son, and Spirit delight in one another and happily work together. Each person in the Trinity has a special role. The Father plans. The Son fulfills the plan of the Father. The Spirit gives life to what the Son does. In eternity past, the Father, Son, and Spirit enjoyed one another so much that they planned to create a world where people could share their happiness. The Father spoke His Word.[9] The Son created according to His Word.[10] The Spirit gave life to what the Son made.[11] The songs and shouts of joy from angels probably reached a pitch of heavenly elation as they delighted in God for completing His marvelous work of creation. Perhaps at this point, pride and jealousy arose in an angel who is now called Satan, and he fell from heaven.[12] Yet even this did not surprise God or threaten His plan to **manifest** His glory—in fact, it served to advance it!

In His matchless wisdom, God designed a way to show His immeasurable love by allowing redeemed sinners to enjoy the fellowship between the Father, Son, and Spirit. Without approving sin or causing it, God allowed Satan to tempt Adam and Eve. God did this so that, through sin and the judgment it brings, He could reveal His amazing love in sending His Son. This love displayed the obedience of His Son to the point of death, even death on a cross.[13] Then He was raised from the dead, ascended into heaven, and given the people for whom He died. This plan was the delight of the Father, Son, and Spirit from all eternity, that they might enable redeemed sinners to enter into their glory.[14] The Father planned to save sinners.[15] The Son became a man to live, die for, and rise in the place of sinners.[16] The Spirit applies the saving work of the Son to sinners.[17] All three persons in the Godhead work together to manifest their beauty and display their worth, so redeemed sinners may be happy in God, and God may be all in all.

Notes

1 Exodus 3:14

2 Acts 17:25

3 Matthew 28:19; John 10:30

4 Proverbs 8:30; John 1:1

5 Isaiah 42:1; Matthew 3:17; John 3:35

6 John 14:31; 17:4

7 John 16:14

8 Proverbs 8:31

9 Hebrews 11:3

10 Colossians 1:16

11 Genesis 1:2

12 Ezekiel 28:12–19; Luke 10:18

13 Philippians 2:8

14 John 17:22

15 Ephesians 1:4

16 Romans 5:8

17 Titus 3:5–6

3

Most Beautiful and Blessed
God, the Source of All Happiness

In Your presence is fullness of joy;
In Your right hand
there are pleasures forever.

— *Psalm* 16:11

Dear children, what is the most beautiful thing you can imagine? Do you like to look at dazzling rainbows and shiny jewels? The Bible says God's throne is surrounded by a rainbow that sparkles like an emerald.[1] It tells of a city with pearl gates that has brilliant stones as its foundation. In the city is a gold street that is so pure it looks like glass. In fact, the entire city is made of gold![2] A crystal clear river flows from God's throne throughout the city. Trees bear all kinds of delicious fruit.[3]

It is possible that the heavenly city really will be made of glistening gems and delightful fruit, and gold will be as common as the dirt we walk on. But it is also possible that God uses the images of gold, sparkling jewels, and luscious fruit to show us how costly, rare, and desirable it is to dwell in His presence.[4] He uses the most treasured items on earth to show the greater treasure of being with Him in heaven. The apostle Paul received a vision of heaven. He said that there are sights and sounds in heaven too wonderful for words.[5] It is impossible to tell people on earth what heaven is like without using earthly words and images, even though they fall short of describing God's beauty and the pleasure of dwelling with Him there.

God is more brilliant than sparkling jewels and radiant rainbows. Heaven is only beautiful because God is seated there.[6] If God stepped out of heaven, it would be black as night.[7] There is nothing on earth as beautiful as God and the place where His glory dwells.[8] The prophets tried to describe heaven by comparing it to the most beautiful objects on earth. Still, there is simply nothing that can give a full picture of God in His heavenly splendor. We must believe that one glimpse of His face will capture our hearts and make us happier than all earth's treasures put together!

All the beauty you see now is a dim reflection of God and His beauty. Most people see beauty with their physical eyes, but to those who behold God in the Scriptures, His beauty is seen by faith.[9]

King David sought one thing only—to behold God in His beauty.[10] God's beauty is most clearly seen in the person of His Son, Jesus Christ.[11] The best gift God could ever give is the gift of His Son.[12] The Bible says God is love.[13] We know God is love because He sent His Son.[14]

He is the One in whom the Father perfectly delights. He is the One who shows us the Father.[15] He is the One who **reconciles** us to the Father.[16] He is the One in whom we were created to enjoy everlasting pleasure and happiness. We must seek to know God's Son!

Notes

1   Revelation 4:3
2   Revelation 21:18–21
3   Revelation 22:1–2
4   Psalm 16:11
5   2 Corinthians 12:4
6   Revelation 21:22–23; 22:3–5
7   Revelation 22:5
8   Psalm 24:7–8; 26:8
9   Ephesians 1:18;
     2 Corinthians 4:6
10   Psalm 27:4
11   2 Corinthians 4:6
12   John 3:16
13   1 John 4:16
14   Hebrews 1:1
15   Matthew 11:27
16   John 14:6

לא תרצח · אנכי יי

לא תנאף · לא יהיה

לא תגנב · לא תשא

לא תענה · זכור את

לא תחמד · כבר את

PART 2

God's Pronouncement on Sinners

There is only one Lawgiver and Judge, the
One who is able to save and to destroy.

– James 4:12

4

A Place of Judgment
God's Throne

All have sinned.

– *Romans 3:23*

ear children, we saw that God is high and exalted.[1] We got a glimpse of the seraphim trembling before Him. We spoke of the brilliant rainbow around His throne. We mentioned the mysterious four living creatures—one like a lion, one like a calf, one with the face of a man, and one like an eagle. They each have six wings and are full of eyes around and within. They give glory to God.

Do you know what else is before His throne? There are twenty-four elders, clothed in white, with golden crowns.[2] When the twenty-four elders hear the four living creatures give glory to God, they fall down, casting their crowns, saying, "Worthy are You, our Lord and our God, to receive glory and honor and power; for You created all things, and because of Your will they existed, and were created" (Revelation 4:11). All in heaven bow before the Lord in worship. The angels praise Him, obeying the voice of His word.[3]

God sits on His throne as Judge.[4] He is the Majestic Sovereign to whom all people owe obedience. Everyone must give an account to Him for how they have lived.[5] They will be judged by the standard of His Law.[6] The books will be opened, and God will repay them according to their deeds.[7]

Have you ever disobeyed one of God's commands? Satan did, and he was immediately cast out of heaven, having become the chief enemy of God.[8] Dear children, please listen carefully. The Bible says if you have disobeyed one of God's commands, you are guilty of breaking His law and must be judged for your sin.[9]

You might think you are not that bad, but the Bible says, "All have sinned and fall short of the glory of God."[10] God is a good God, worthy of perfect love and obedience. Have you ever told a lie? The penalty for one lie against a high and holy God is punishment under His righteous wrath forever.[11] "But it is just one little lie," you might say. It is not the size of the sin but the worth of the One against whom you have sinned that makes it so terrible. You have not sinned against a man who is your equal or against an angel who is above you, but against the Creator of the universe who made you and takes care of you! Dear children, you must recognize the seriousness of sin.

Notes

1   Isaiah 6:1; 57:15–17

2   Revelation 4:4

3   Psalm 103:20

4   James 4:12

5   Romans 14:12

6   Galatians 3:10

7   Romans 2:6;
    Revelation 20:12–13

8   Luke 10:18

9   James 2:10; Romans 3:19

10   Romans 3:23

11   Exodus 20:16; Colossians 3:9;
     James 2:10; Romans 2:5–6

5

Man's Greatest Problem
God Judges Sinners

The wages of sin is death.
– *Romans 6:23*

*D*ear children, have you ever had a difficult problem? What did you do? Maybe you thought for a long time and came up with an answer. Maybe you worked hard at it and fixed it. Or maybe you got help from your mom or dad. Those are wonderful solutions, but did you know that each of us has a terrible problem we cannot solve? No matter how long we think, how hard we work, or who we ask for help, our problem remains. Do you know what our problem is? It is our sin. Sin is terrible because it is against God, and God is holy, just, and good. Sin is our greatest problem because it makes us be at **enmity** with God. Sin is our own worst enemy because it brings God's wrath upon us.

The Bible says that sin entered the world through Adam, and all his **descendants** sinned in him.[1] This means that each one of us is born spiritually dead in

trespasses and sins.[2] It is our nature to sin against God and do wrong. We do not want to submit to His laws.[3] We do not fear Him or honor Him.[4] We worship (or trust in) the things He has made rather than Him, our Maker.[5] We are children of disobedience.[6]

Worse yet, our pride blinds us from recognizing our desperate condition. Just as Adam and Eve sewed fig leaves to try to cover their shame, so we try to cover our sin by pretending that we are good—but God sees right through. He knows who we really are. We continue to profess our own righteousness, but God says it is like filthy rags.[7]

Dear children, I do not say this to hurt you but to help you see your need for a Savior—only then can you know and rejoice in God's love! But before we focus on God's love, we need to learn more about our sinful condition. God's love for us shines most brightly against the backdrop of our sin.[8]

The seed of every sin resides in our hearts. We are capable of the worst sins because our hearts are sinful to the core. Our hearts are full of greed, and we will steal if God does not help us. Our hearts are full of hate, and we will murder if God does not intervene. Our hearts are full of pride, and we would even try to sit on God's throne if possible. In our natural state, we are lovers of self, lovers of money, boastful, arrogant, revilers, disobedient to parents, ungrateful, unholy, unloving, **irreconcilable**, cruel gossips, without self-control, brutal, haters of good, treacherous, reckless, conceited, and lovers of pleasure rather than lovers of God.[9]

That is a long list of sins, isn't it? You might say that you have not done all those things. But the Bible says your heart is corrupt enough to do them and, if God does not hold you back, you will do them.

Now, dear children, I want you to think about the worst sin of all, from which all other sins flow. Do you know what that is? The worst sin of all is to not love God's Son.[10] God has set forth His beauty in His Son that all might delight in Him, giving Him the glory due His name. But instead, the Bible says that people hated Him. They thought He deserved to suffer. They agreed that He should be crucified.[11] You might think, how could they do that? Yet every sin we commit shows that we have done the same thing. Yes, our sin placed Him on the cross because we love lawlessness and do not want to obey God. Every act of disobedience proves this is true.

Sin is not just breaking a rule—sin is breaking **covenant** relationship with God. God's laws are the terms of His covenant relationship. To break His law is to say, "I don't want to be in a covenant relationship with you. I don't want you to be my God, and I don't want to be one of your people." This explains why sinners are enemies of God.[12] They don't want God and His laws. Instead, they want to create their own laws. They want to control their own lives. They want to serve themselves. They want everyone to say how great they are instead of how great God is! They don't want to bow before God—they want others to bow before them! This is what Satan wanted—he wanted

God's glory for himself, and the mere thought of it was enough to justly condemn him forever. This is what every descendant of Adam wants too.

What is the punishment for sin? Every sin deserves God's wrath and curse.[13] There is nothing more dreadful than the wrath of God. While sinners live under God's wrath to some degree during this life,[14] the Bible speaks of a wrath to come.[15] Have you ever stored up something for yourself? Maybe you stored up money. Every time you got a little bit of money, you put it away until you finally had such a large amount that you could buy what you wanted. Storing up wrath for ourselves is something like that, but we are not storing up something good. We are storing up something bad.[16] Every sin we commit is increasing our storehouse of God's wrath.[17] On the day of judgment, it will fall upon us in full force if we have not **repented** of our sins and trusted in Christ. God's wrath is so horrible that people would rather be crushed by mountains than face it.[18] Worse yet, it goes on forever and ever.

Dear children, do you recognize that you are a sinner? Do you know you have sinned against the God who made you and takes care of you, who is good and kind beyond all measure? Do you know that upon your death, God will judge you for every sin you have committed? Do you realize that God's justice requires that He do so? Do you desire a way to be saved from His judgment and wrath? He has provided a way!

Notes

1 Romans 5:12

2 Ephesians 2:1–2

3 Romans 8:7

4 Romans 1:21; 3:18

5 Romans 1:23

6 Ephesians 2:2; 5:6

7 Isaiah 64:6

8 This thought is taken from Paul Washer.

9 2 Timothy 3:2–4

10 John 3:36; 5:23. Those who have never heard the name of Jesus must still give an account to God for their sin since He has made Himself known through creation (Romans 1:19–20). They are guilty of breaking His law, which is written on their hearts (Romans 2:14–16), and of failing to give Him glory (Romans 1:18, 21). But those who have been given the knowledge of salvation through faith in Jesus Christ and do not repent and believe will face a stricter judgment for disobeying the light God has given them.

11 Isaiah 53:3–4

12 Romans 5:10

13 Question 84 of the Westminster Shorter Catechism and Question 89 of the Baptist Shorter Catechism. See Galatians 3:10; Romans 1:18; 2:5–6.

14 John 3:36; Romans 1:18; Ephesians 2:3

15 Matthew 3:7; Romans 2:5–6; 4:15; 5:9; Ephesians 5:6; Colossians 3:6; 1 Thessalonians 1:10

16 God's wrath itself is not bad; rather, it is just and pure because it is part of His holy nature. But to be the recipient of God's wrath due to our sin is a terrifying thing (Hebrews 10:31).

17 1 Thessalonians 2:16

18 Revelation 6:16

6

A Shocking Provision
God Sends His Son

When the fullness of the time came,
God sent forth His Son.

– Galatians 4:4

od is just, and He is right to judge sinners. The seraphim and angels rejoice to see His glory **vindicated**. But in His matchless wisdom, God devised a way to be just and justify sinners, so He can show mercy by forgiving them and receiving them as His beloved children. This is a salvation over which angels marvel.[1] This is a love that cannot be measured![2] How could a just and holy God receive sinful rebels as His beloved children? The answer is through the sinless one who bears His wrath in their place.[3]

The sinless one must be a man who is holy, blameless, and righteous. He must live every second of his life to glorify the Father. He must find all his delight in the Father and in doing His will. He must keep the terms of the covenant perfectly, never once disobeying God's law. Moreover, he must be a friend of God who is willing to be treated as an enemy. He must have unlimited strength so He can endure God's wrath without being destroyed. He must be of infinite value—that means a value so large it cannot be measured—because a God of infinite value requires an infinite punishment for sin.[4] The only way for sinners to be spared from an infinite punishment is by punishing something of infinite value in their place.

Yet, all Adam's descendants are born in sin.[5] No one is righteous.[6] No one lives to glorify the Father. No one perfectly obeys His law. There is no sinless person. Moreover, no one has infinite value because all created beings are **finite**. No one could endure the wrath of the Father without being destroyed. There is no sacrifice that could pay the debt we owe because it is an infinite debt due to the infinite worth of the One against whom we have sinned. No one is worthy.[7]

Why couldn't God have made another man without sin, like Adam, to be the sin-bearer? He could have made another man, but this man would not have been qualified to save the descendants of Adam because he would not *be* a descendant of Adam. Therefore, his righteousness could not be credited to the descendants of Adam, nor would he be qualified to suffer the penalty for their sins. Even if God created another man in the likeness of Adam, that man would still be a finite creature. He would not be able to suffer God's wrath without being destroyed, nor would his sacrifice be of infinite value and acceptable to God.[8]

There is only one who is sinless and who could bear the wrath of the Father. There is only one who could pay off an infinite debt by His infinite worth. There is only one who finds all His delight in the Father and in doing His will. It is God's own Son. In the eternal plan of God, the Father chose to send His Son—the Son in whom He delighted for all eternity—to take His people's sins and suffer God's wrath in their place.[9] But if God is spirit, how could He obey and suffer as a man?

In the fullness of time, God sent forth His Son to be born as a man.[10] He was **conceived** by the Holy Spirit in the womb of the Virgin Mary, being a true descendant of Adam.[11] He was fully human, like us, but without sin because He is God.[12] The angel Gabriel said that His name should be Jesus because He would save His people from their sins.[13] He was a holy, sinless, righteous descendant of Adam from the moment He was conceived.

When the Son of God became a man, He remained fully God. He did not lose any of His **deity**. Instead, He added humanity to His deity and became the God-man. Some of His divine glory was hidden by the veil of human flesh, but it was all still there. As the God-man, He was the only qualified descendant of Adam who could save sinners.

Do you think it was nothing for the Son of God to leave the worship of angels and seraphim? Do you think it was a small thing for the immortal God to humble Himself by taking on human flesh? Do you think it was easy to enter a world where most people would not recognize Him as God? It required amazing humility.[14] These things were costly to the Son, but do you know what cost Him most of all? It wasn't leaving the worship of heaven or assuming the likeness of sinful flesh or even entering a sinful world.[15] What cost Him most was leaving the presence of His Father in whom He delighted. Remember how the Father and Son enjoyed perfect fellowship for all eternity, finding their pleasure in one another? Can you imagine the sacrifice the Son made when He stepped out of the Father's presence? He left that place of sweet fellowship to enter a world where men hated Him and His Father.[16] His fellowship with the Father continued, but as through a veil. For a time, He made Himself lower than angels who openly beheld His Father's face while He did not.[17] Imagine the shock of angels as they saw their Lord lower Himself to become a man, born under the curse to save sinners.

The reason the Son left the presence of His Father was to please His Father. He said, "A body You have prepared for Me. . . . I have come to do Your will" (Hebrews 10:5, 7). He left the glories of heaven and the sweet communion with His Father to honor His Father by laying down His life to save sinners.[18]

Notes

1   1 Peter 1:12

2   Ephesians 3:18–19

3   Romans 5:8–9;
     2 Corinthians 5:21

4   This thought comes from
     Puritan author John Flavel.

5   Romans 5:12

6   Romans 3:10

7   Revelation 5:4

8   There are several reasons for this: (1) redeemed sinners would not receive the adoption as sons and all the privileges that come from being in the Son, for only the Son of God, and no other created being, can elevate redeemed sinners to the position He has with the Father; (2) another man, albeit sinless, would not have a position with the Father to enable Him to bring sinners near—they might be forgiven but would still be kept at a distance. They might be delivered from punishment but would not be objects of His peculiar love; (3) God's own Son would not receive the eternal glory of being the Savior of sinners, which is at the heart of the plan of salvation; (4) to have created another man for the sole purpose of suffering in the place of sinners would have required no sacrifice on God's part. Therefore, His immeasurable love through the giving of His only begotten Son would not be on display.

9   Acts 2:23; 1 John 4:10

10   Galatians 4:4

11   Luke 1:27–33

12   Hebrews 4:15; 7:26;
     1 Peter 2:22; 1 John 3:5

13   Matthew 1:21

14   Philippians 2:6–8

15   "For what the Law could not do, weak as it was through the flesh, God did: sending His own Son in the likeness of sinful flesh" (Romans 8:3). Paul Washer explains, "The phrase 'likeness of sinful flesh' does not mean the body of Jesus was sinful. The body of Jesus was holy and pure. However, it does mean His body bore the consequences of sin. His body was not like the body of Adam before the fall; rather, it was a body weakened by the fall."

16   John 15:18, 23

17   Hebrews 2:7

18   John 10:17

PART 3

Jesus's Birth and Childhood

You shall call His name Jesus, for He will
save His people from their sins.

– *Matthew 1:21*

7

God Made Flesh

Jesus the Son of God

The Word became flesh,
and dwelt among us.

— *John 1:14*

D ear children, where do you think would be a good place for a king to be born? Maybe in a beautiful palace? Do you think he would have a lavish nursery full of plush toys and fancy furniture? Do you picture him being rocked in a satin-lined cradle and adorned with a little royal robe? Do you imagine servants attending to his every want and need?

Do you know where the Son of God was born as a man? He was born in a barn. He slept in the trough from which animals ate. He was wrapped in rags. There were no toys, furniture, or servants. Isn't this surprising? Why didn't earth rightly receive its King? Why did God allow His Son to be born in such lowliness? The humiliation of being born in such circumstances dimly pictures the **condescension** of the Son of God leaving the glory of heaven to be born as a man under the curse. It tells us something about the cost and the astonishing nature of His **incarnation**. It is shocking and unfitting, yet it speaks of the immeasurable love of God and the great depths to which He stooped to save sinners.

Near the barn where Jesus lay, shepherds were watching their sheep by night. Then,

> an angel of the Lord suddenly stood before them, and the glory of the Lord shone around them; and they were terribly frightened. But the angel said to them, "Do not be afraid; for behold, I bring you good news of great joy which will be for all the people; for today in the city of David there has been born for you a Savior, who is Christ the Lord. This will be a sign for you: you will find a baby wrapped in cloths and lying in a manger." And suddenly there appeared with the angel a multitude of the heavenly host praising God and saying, "Glory to God in the highest, and on earth peace among men with whom He is pleased." (Luke 2:9–14)

What is this "good news of great joy"? It is the provision God made to save sinners through His Son! There is no greater news—there is no greater joy!

The angel told the shepherds that Jesus was born in "the city of David," which is Bethlehem. Why was Jesus born in the ordinary town of Bethlehem? Wouldn't He have been born in the glorious city of Jerusalem, where all the kings of Judah lived and where the temple stood? Jesus was born in Bethlehem to fulfill this **prophecy**: "But as for you, Bethlehem . . . One will go forth for Me to be ruler in Israel. His goings forth are from . . . eternity" (Micah 5:2). The name Bethlehem means "house of bread." Do you know why Jesus was born in a town with that name? It is because He is the Bread of Life![1] Just as bread gives life to our bodies, so Jesus's death on the cross gives eternal life to our souls. Because of His death and resurrection, we can have eternal life if we repent of our sins and trust in Him.

The place of Jesus's birth verifies that He is from the line of King David, who was also from Bethlehem. It shows that He is the fulfillment of the promise God made to King David, that one of his offspring would sit on the throne as King forever. The only one who could reign forever is one who is eternal—that is God's Son!

The angels not only bore witness to Jesus's birth, but they praised God for His love in sending His Son to save sinners. It is a love that is mysterious to them. They are not the recipients of it, yet they glorify God for His greatness displayed in it!

Notes

1   John 6:35

8

God's Greatest Gift
Jesus the King Is Born

We have come to worship Him.

— *Matthew 2:2*

*E*ight days after His birth, Jesus was circumcised and officially given the name Jesus, which means "Savior." In keeping with the law of Moses, Mary and Joseph waited another thirty-three days to present Him to the Lord in Jerusalem.[1] Where do you think they stayed during those thirty-three days? The Gospel of Matthew says they were in a house in Bethlehem.[2] It is possible they lodged with distant relatives or found temporary housing with another family while they waited to present Jesus to the Lord.

Mary and Joseph brought Jesus to Jerusalem when the thirty-three days were completed. According to the law of Moses, they were required to sacrifice a year-old lamb as a burnt **offering** and a turtledove as a sin offering in place of their first-born son. If they could not afford a lamb, they were permitted to offer two pigeons or two turtledoves instead. In accordance with God's law, Mary and Joseph offered two turtledoves and presented Jesus to the Lord.[3] Thirty-three years later, this same Jesus would present Himself to the Lord as a sin offering in Mary's and Joseph's place and that of many others.[4]

While Mary, Joseph, and baby Jesus were in the temple, they met a man named Simeon. He was a righteous man, looking for God's promise of salvation. When Simeon saw Jesus, the Holy Spirit opened his eyes to recognize Him as the Savior. He took Jesus into his arms and said, "For my eyes have seen Your salvation, which You have prepared in the presence of all peoples" (Luke 2:30–31). At that moment, Anna the prophetess, who served in the temple night and day with fasting and prayer, came over and began giving thanks to God. She continually talked about Jesus to all who were looking for God's **salvation**.[5] Then Simeon turned to Mary. He said that her son would be opposed by many, and a sword would pierce her soul—speaking of the pain she would feel when she witnessed Jesus's death on the cross.[6] Through Simeon, God **testified** that the child was born to die—that He alone is the righteous one who is qualified to save sinners.

Most likely, about this time, **magi** came, as the Scripture reads, "Now after Jesus was born in Bethlehem of Judea in the days of Herod the king, magi from the east arrived in Jerusalem" (Matthew 2:1). God had placed a star in the sky as a sign. The magi understood it to be God's announcement that "the King is born!"

They wanted to worship Him, so they followed the star. Remember, though Jesus was King, He was not yet reigning in His human body as King. He was just a baby! Yet, by faith, the magi recognized Him as King and went to worship Him. Like the magi, though we do not yet see Jesus ruling in His human body, we are to recognize Him as King and worship Him.

It would have taken the magi months to travel to Jerusalem. They would have faced treacherous mountains, dangerous rivers, vast deserts, and wild animals. They would have been in danger of thieves and overcome with exhaustion. Yet they esteemed Him worthy and found no price too high to come and worship Him.

Once they arrived in Jerusalem, they said, "Where is He who has been born King of the Jews? For we saw His star in the east and have come to worship Him" (Matthew 2:2). When they learned that He was in Bethlehem, they traveled there. The star led them to the place where Jesus was staying, and "they rejoiced exceedingly with great joy" (Matthew 2:10). When they came into the house, they fell down before Him and worshiped. They gave Him gifts of gold, frankincense, and myrrh, trading their earthly treasures for heavenly ones, counting Him to be their greatest treasure.[7]

Then an angel of the Lord spoke to Joseph in a dream, telling him to take Jesus and Mary to Egypt.[8] Joseph immediately obeyed. Very soon afterward, King Herod murdered all the baby boys in Bethlehem who were two years old and under, hoping that one of them was Jesus. He had become jealous when he learned that the magi had come to worship Jesus.[9] But God cannot be tricked. His plan cannot be ruined! God made provision to protect His Son that the prophecy might be fulfilled, "Out of Egypt I called My Son" (Matthew 2:15).

After King Herod died, an angel appeared to Joseph again and told him to return to Israel.[10] So Joseph, Mary, and Jesus settled back in Nazareth of Galilee that the prophecy might be fulfilled, "He shall be called a Nazarene" (Matthew 2:23).

Notes

1   Leviticus 12:6–8

2   Matthew 2:8–11

3   Luke 2:22–24

4   Galatians 1:4

5   Luke 2:38

6   Though Mary would experience grief while witnessing Jesus's crucifixion, it was the sword that pierced Jesus that revealed the thoughts of many hearts.

7   Matthew 2:11

8   Matthew 2:13

9   Matthew 2:16–18

10   Matthew 2:20

9

An Obedient Son
Jesus's Childhood

Did you not know that I had
to be in My Father's house?

– Luke 2:49

*J*esus lived a humble, ordinary life. But there was one thing about Him that was different. Do you know what it was? He never sinned![1] As a five-year-old, as a ten-year-old, as a fifteen-year-old, He perfectly loved the Father with all His heart, soul, mind, and strength and kept His commands.[2] He looked like every other child on the outside, but His whole nature and all His desires were set on loving and obeying His heavenly Father. As His body developed and His mind matured, He expressed His love and obedience in more visible ways. As soon as He was able to speak, He was probably found in prayer, with hands lifted and praise songs on His lips. As a small child, He most likely listened well at **synagogue** and participated during family worship. Once He could read, He probably spent unusual amounts of time in the Scriptures.

He was an honoring son—obedient, respectful, dependable, and hardworking. He was a caring and forgiving big brother. Even as a child, He showed the fruit of the Spirit. He was a loving, joyful, peaceful, patient, kind, good, faithful, gentle, and self-controlled little boy.[3] He was marked by holiness, perfectly keeping God's law. But what set Him apart more than anything was His love for His Father in heaven.

At age twelve, Jesus accompanied His parents to Jerusalem for the annual **Passover** celebration.[4] The entire village of Nazareth would have journeyed together, most likely on foot. The adults probably talked as they walked while the children ran circles around them, laughing and playing, or possibly even running ahead of their parents, full of excitement. It would not have been unusual for the parents to walk several hours, deep in conversation, without paying much attention to the youngsters who were happily leading the way.

The Bible says that Jesus continued to grow in wisdom and **stature**.[5] It might have been at age twelve when Jesus realized, in His human nature, that He was to be the Passover Lamb. This might explain why His parents found Him asking and answering questions in the temple when they were looking for Him.

Do you think His questions were about the meaning of the Passover and its fulfillment in the Savior? Is it possible He was seeking to understand the meaning of passages like Isaiah 53, and as He discussed it with the teachers, the Spirit revealed to Him that He was the Passover Lamb?

Can you imagine what He might have felt as a twelve-year-old when He realized He was to suffer His Father's wrath in the place of sinners? There is no doubt that His heart overflowed with love for the people He was to save, yet He must have had a seriousness about Him that was way beyond His years.

After celebrating the Passover, His parents began their journey back to Bethlehem, assuming that Jesus was traveling with the group. Yet Jesus remained in Jerusalem. At some point, His parents noticed that He was missing. While Jesus might have been realizing that He was the Passover Lamb, His parents were frantically looking for Him. Three days later, they found Him in the temple. Bewildered, His mother asked why He would treat them this way, suggesting that He should have been with the young people traveling to Nazareth instead of the teachers in the temple.[6] Jesus answered, "Why is it that you were looking for Me? Did you not know that I had to be in My Father's house?" (Luke 2:49). Though His parents did not understand, Jesus was affirming His identity as the Son of God and His purpose to be about His Father's business.[7] Even as a boy, **zeal** for His Father's house **consumed** Him.[8] His parents could count on finding Him with the Father and need not look elsewhere.

This might have been the time Jesus set His heart to prepare for the cross. Most sons began preparation for their life work at age twelve. How much more might Jesus have begun to prepare for the cross at age twelve? How would He have done this? While we know He assisted His earthly father with his trade, He probably spent the rest of His time wrestling in prayer and memorizing Scripture. Does twenty-one years sound like a long time to pray for one's life call? It's not too long if that call is to bear the sins of the people He has loved for all eternity. As the Spirit revealed the suffering to come, we can imagine He must have agonized in prayer to do His Father's will. Most likely, while other young boys were romping about, Jesus was disciplining Himself for the cross. While other boys were socializing, Jesus was studying and memorizing Scripture. While other young men were starting their trades, Jesus was wrestling with the enemy. While other young men were pursuing a wife, Jesus was preparing for His bride, the church.[9] While other men were raising their children, Jesus was interceding for the children the Father would give Him.[10] While other men were seeking the things of this world, Jesus was seeking the things above. While other men were preparing for life, Jesus was preparing to die.

He was an ordinary boy on the outside, but everything on the inside was sinless, holy, and devoted to His Father. He was the express image of the invisible God and the exact representation of His nature.[11] He was a young man marked by love, and for the joy set before Him, He prepared for the cross.[12]

Notes

1. 1 John 3:5
2. Mark 12:30
3. Galatians 5:22–23
4. Luke 2:41–43
5. Luke 2:52
6. Luke 2:48
7. John 4:34
8. John 2:17
9. Revelation 19:7–9
10. Hebrews 2:13
11. Hebrews 1:3
12. Hebrews 12:2

PART 4

Jesus's Messianic Ministry

Jesus was going through all the cities
and villages, teaching in their synagogues
and proclaiming the gospel of the kingdom,
and healing every kind of disease
and every kind of sickness.

– Matthew 9:35

10

Behold the Lamb
Jesus's Baptism, Temptation, and Teaching

This is My beloved Son,
in whom I am well-pleased.

– Matthew 3:17

*J*esus continued to prepare for the cross throughout His young adult years. When He was thirty years old, the Father called Him to begin His messianic ministry. When John the Baptist saw Jesus, he said, "Behold, the Lamb of God who takes away the sin of the world!" (John 1:29). To most, Jesus looked like an ordinary man, but the Spirit caused some people to recognize Him as the Son of God.

In obedience to the Father, Jesus was baptized. Though He had no sin to repent of, His baptism was fitting to fulfill all righteousness.[1] He humbled Himself to identify with sinners, initiating baptism as a sign of the covenant He was to make with His people through the cross. His baptism pictured His death, burial, and resurrection.[2] When He came up out of the water, the heavens opened, and the Spirit of God descended upon Him like a dove.[3] A voice came out of the heavens saying, "This is My beloved Son, in whom I am well-pleased" (Matthew 3:17). Both the Father and the Spirit testified that Jesus is the Son of God and the Savior of sinners.

After Jesus's baptism, the Spirit led Him into the wilderness to be tempted by the devil.[4] Did you ever wonder why God led Him there? It was to prepare Him for the cross by training Him to resist temptation. It was to test His obedience and prove His sinlessness. It was to affirm His humanity and make Him like us in all things. It was to make Him a merciful Savior who could sympathize with His people in their weakness.[5] It was to glorify the Father by proving His invincible love for Him. In the wilderness, Jesus did in the worst conditions what Adam could not do in the best conditions. Jesus did what no human could do—He remained sinless.

After His temptation, Jesus began to preach, saying, "Repent, for the kingdom of heaven is at hand" (Matthew 4:17). He went about all the cities and villages, teaching in their synagogues, proclaiming the gospel, and healing every kind of sickness and disease.[6] As a result, multitudes followed Him.

When Jesus taught, the crowds were amazed because He taught with authority.[7] He taught on true blessedness and the purpose of the law.[8] He taught that we are to seek God's approval, not the approval of people. He said that our acts of love and devotion, such as giving, praying, and fasting, are to be done in secret for God to see, and He will reward us.[9]

Jesus taught that we are to store our treasures in heaven, not on earth, because we cannot love both God and money.[10] He said that it is easier for a camel to go through the eye of a needle than for a rich man to enter heaven.[11] God knows what we need and is able to provide for us. We are not to worry. We are to seek God, not food, clothes, and earthly things. If we seek first His kingdom and His righteousness, He will provide everything we need.[12]

Jesus taught that instead of focusing on other people's sins, we are to focus on getting rid of our own sin. Then we can help others with their sin.[13] But we need to do it with love and humility, remembering that we are sinners too.

Jesus taught that we are to pray, pray, pray, and keep on praying![14] The Father delights in giving good gifts to those who ask.[15]

Jesus taught that the way to heaven is difficult, and few find it, while the way to hell is easy, and many go that way.[16] He said that we must take all measures to keep ourselves from sin because it leads to hell, where the fire is not quenched.[17]

Not everyone who says to Jesus, "Lord, Lord," will enter the kingdom of heaven.[18] Many say that they believe. They preach in His name and claim to do good deeds, but they do not know Him. On that final day, He will tell them, "I never knew you; depart from Me, you who practice lawlessness" (Matthew 7:23). True believers are the ones who know Him and love Him more than anything. They build their lives on His Word.[19] Jesus warned that there will be false believers who will try to lead many astray. He said we will be able to recognize them by their fruit.[20] Jesus said that the one who does the will of His Father in heaven is the one who belongs to God,[21] and the most important work of all is to believe in Jesus Christ, whom God has sent.[22]

Jesus often spoke to the multitudes in parables, which are stories that teach spiritual truths. Most of His parables were about the kingdom of heaven. He compared the kingdom of heaven to a pearl of great price and a hidden treasure.[23] He taught that we should value the kingdom of heaven above earthly things and be willing to lose all to gain it. He also taught parables on repentance, forgiveness, love, prayer, humility, stewardship, God's pursuit of sinners, and His second coming.

Notes

1   Matthew 3:15–16

2   Colossians 2:12

3   Matthew 3:16

4   Matthew 4:1

5   Hebrews 2:17–18; 4:15

6   Matthew 4:23

7   Matthew 7:29

8   Matthew 5:1–16, 17–48

9   Matthew 6:1–18

10   Matthew 6:19–24

11   Matthew 19:24

12   Matthew 6:25–34

13   Matthew 7:1–5

14   Matthew 7:7–12; Luke 18:1–8

15   Matthew 7:11

16   Matthew 7:13–14

17   Mark 9:44

18   Matthew 7:21

19   Matthew 7:24–27

20   Matthew 7:15–20

21   Matthew 12:50

22   John 6:28–29

23   Matthew 13:1–52

11

Follow Me
Jesus's Call to Discipleship

He who does not take his cross and
follow after Me is not worthy of Me.

– Matthew 10:38

esus called all people to follow Him, but there were certain men He called in particular. Peter was one of those men. When Peter and his brother Andrew were fishing, Jesus told them to lower their nets. Peter reluctantly said, "Master, we worked hard all night and caught nothing, but I will do as You say and let down the nets" (Luke 5:5).

Immediately, so many fish swam into the net that it began to tear. When James and John helped him pull in the fish, there were so many fish that the boat began to sink!

Convicted by his unbelief, Peter fell at Jesus's feet, saying, "Go away from me Lord, for I am a sinful man!" (Luke 5:8). Jesus said to him, "Do not fear, from now on you will be catching men" (Luke 5:10). "Follow Me, and

I will make you fishers of men" (Matthew 4:19). Do you know what Jesus meant by "fishers of men"? Instead of bringing fish into his net, Peter would be bringing people into God's kingdom. Instead of spending his life fishing, he would spend it preaching the gospel. This was Peter's call to the ministry. Through the fish, Jesus showed that Peter's ministry would be bountiful and blessed!

Including Peter, Jesus called twelve men to be His apostles.[1] He sent them to the cities and villages to preach.[2] He entrusted them with the mysteries of God's kingdom.[3] He walked with them for three years. He taught them the hidden meanings of the parables.[4] He revealed to them the mystery of the Trinity.[5] He showed them the way to eternal life.[6] He made them His close friends.[7] He trained them to be His witnesses.[8] He **commissioned** them to make disciples of all nations.[9]

Jesus had other disciples too. He sent out seventy men to teach about the kingdom of God, calling people everywhere to repent.[10] Though others claimed to be His disciples, some of them fell away. They stopped following Him because they thought His teachings were too hard.[11]

Several women were among Jesus's disciples. They accompanied Him as He preached throughout the villages. They ministered to His needs and supported Him financially; among these women were Mary Magdalene, Joanna, and Susanna.[12] In addition, Jesus's earthly mother and the mother of James and John followed

Him.[13] These women were given a special role in being the first to see Him in His resurrected body and to testify of His resurrection.[14]

The cost of discipleship is high, but Jesus is worth it. Jesus said that those who follow Him will be delivered up to kings and governors for His sake as a testimony. Their own family members will deliver them over to death. They will be hated by all on account of His name, but the one who endures to the end will be saved.[15]

Jesus taught that whoever **confesses** Him before men, He will confess before His Father in heaven; but whoever denies Him before men, He will deny before His Father in heaven. He who does not love Jesus more than father, mother, brother, son, or daughter is not worthy of Him.[16]

The one who wants to be Jesus's disciple must deny himself, take up his cross, and follow Jesus. For whoever wishes to save his life shall lose it, but he who loses his life for Jesus's sake shall find it. For what will it profit a man if he gains the whole world but loses his soul?[17] However, if he loses the world and gains Christ, he is the richest of all because Jesus is the true and only treasure worth seeking.

Jesus said that many who are first will be last, and the last, first.[18] Whoever exalts himself will be humbled, but he who humbles himself will be exalted.[19] The greatest will be a servant, and whoever wishes to be first must be a slave, just as Jesus did not come to be served but to serve and to give His life as a ransom for many.[20]

Does this teaching sound too hard? It is hard, but the price of not following Jesus is one we cannot afford. Jesus said that we are to do whatever we must to avoid sin.[21] Jesus said not to fear man who can kill the body, but to fear God who can destroy both body and soul in hell.[22]

What is the reward for those who are faithful? Everyone who has left houses, brothers or sisters, father or mother, children, or farms for His name's sake will receive many times as much and will inherit eternal life.[23] If you say, "That's all?" then you do not know how wonderful God is and how much happiness is to be found in His presence! Jesus said eternal life is to know the Father and the Son.[24] This is the greatest reward known to man—to dwell in the love of the Father and the Son. The love of all men and angels put together is nothing compared to the love of God revealed in His Son!

Notes

1   Matthew 10:2–4
2   Mark 3:14
3   Mark 4:10–11
4   Mark 4:33–34
5   John 14:16–26
6   John 14:6
7   John 15:14–15
8   Acts 1:8
9   Matthew 28:18–20
10 Luke 10:1
11 John 6:59–66
12 Matthew 27:55–56; Luke 8:1–3
13 Matthew 27:61; John 19:25
14 Matthew 28:1, 7

15 Matthew 10:18, 21–22
16 Matthew 10:32–33, 37
17 Matthew 10:38–39; 16:24, 26
18 Matthew 19:30
19 Matthew 23:12
20 Matthew 20:28
21 Matthew 5:29–30
22 Matthew 10:28
23 Matthew 19:29
24 John 17:3

12

God's Servant
Jesus's Wisdom, Power, and Miracles

Behold, My Servant, whom I uphold;
My chosen one in whom My soul delights.
I have put My Spirit upon Him.

– Isaiah 42:1

esus had power over all creation because He was perfectly obedient to the will of God and anointed by the Spirit without measure. He rebuked the winds and waves, and they obeyed Him.[1] He fed over five thousand men with only five loaves of bread and two fish and had twelve baskets full of left-overs![2] He turned water into wine, appointed a multitude of fish to swim into Peter's net, and caused a coin to be found in a fish's mouth.[3] He cursed a fig tree and it withered, put a man's ear back on his head, and healed a bleeding woman.[4] He even walked on water![5] He caused the lame to walk, gave sight to the blind, made the dumb to speak, cleansed the lepers, and raised people from the dead.[6] He had authority over evil spirits and cast them out.[7] He commanded evil spirits not to speak, and they obeyed.[8] The multitudes were amazed. The miracles He performed testified that He is the Son of God.[9]

Many initially believed in Him but found the cost of discipleship too high and fell away.[10] Others followed Him because of the free food and exciting miracles but quickly left when they heard His teaching.[11] Still, others were hoping He would be the political savior to deliver them from Rome, only later to cry out, "Crucify Him!"[12] Only a few followed Him because they recognized Him to be the Son of God.[13]

The multitudes were not the only ones to notice Jesus's miracles. The religious leaders, especially a group called the Pharisees, also noticed, and they were jealous.[14] Instead of rejoicing that God had sent His Son to save sinners—such as themselves—they were angry that sinners began to follow Jesus instead of following them!

They plotted and schemed to find a way to get rid of Jesus. They tried to seize Him but were afraid because the multitudes respected Him as a prophet.[15] So they tried to trick Him. But Jesus cannot be tricked! When they accused Him of associating with sinners, He told them it is not those who are healthy who need a doctor but those who are sick; for He did not come to call the so-called righteous but sinners to repentance.[16]

They thought they could trap Him by asking if it was lawful to pay taxes to Caesar.[17] If He said yes, the

Jews would stone Him for **treason**. If He said no, the Romans would charge Him with **insurrection**. Jesus said, "Give me a coin." Looking at it, He asked them, "Whose image is this?" They answered, "Caesar's." Jesus said, "Render to Caesar the things that are Caesar's; and to God the things that are God's" (Matthew 22:18–22). The Pharisees marveled at His wisdom and dared not ask Him any more questions.

Jesus kept preaching, teaching, and healing. He was moved with compassion because He saw the people were distressed and downcast, like sheep without a shepherd.[18] When He entered the village of Bethany, He stayed at the house of a man named Lazarus, who had two sisters, Mary and Martha. Martha was busy making dinner while Mary was sitting at Jesus's feet, listening to Him speak. Martha felt angry that she was serving alone while Mary was spending time with Jesus. It did not seem fair! She came out of the kitchen and told Jesus to rebuke Mary. But Jesus rebuked Martha instead! He told her that she was worried and bothered about so many things but that only one thing was necessary. He said Mary had made the better choice.[19] The better choice is to spend time with Jesus, listening to His Word.

Jesus continued to seek His Father during His messianic ministry. He rose early in the morning to pray.[20] Sometimes He prayed all night![21] He walked in dependence on the Spirit to maintain communion with the Father and do His will. He longed to accomplish His Father's work through the cross so He could triumphantly return to His Father's presence, bringing His people with Him.

During the Passover, Jesus entered the temple and cast out all who were buying and selling. He overturned the tables of the moneychangers and drove out those who were selling doves. He said, "It is written, 'My house shall be called a house of prayer'; but you are making it a robbers' den" (Matthew 21:13). He also said, "Take these things away; stop making My Father's house a place of business" (John 2:16). His disciples remembered that it was written of the **Messiah** in the Old Testament, "Zeal for Your house will consume Me" (John 2:17). Jesus was rightly jealous for His Father's glory, being justly angered by those seeking to make money from the worship of God.

The Pharisees had heard enough. When Jesus told them His Father is working and He Himself is working, they sought to kill Him because He was calling God His own Father, making Himself equal with God.[22] They refused to acknowledge Jesus as God. Knowing their thoughts, Jesus told them the Father loved Him and showed Him all the Father was doing. He said that just as the Father gives life, so He gives life. He said that the Father has given all judgment to the Son that all may honor the Son as they honor the Father. Whoever does not honor the Son does not honor the Father who sent Him. But whoever hears His Word and believes in Him has eternal life. He will not be judged but will pass from death to life.[23]

Then, Jesus began to speak publicly of His crucifixion.[24] He said that when He was "lifted up," all people would know that He was from the Father.[25] The crowds did not understand what He meant by this.

In private, Jesus told His disciples plainly that He must go to Jerusalem to suffer at the hands of the religious leaders, be killed, and then be raised up on the third day.[26] The twelve disciples did not believe that Jesus would be killed or raised—but Mary of Bethany did. When Jesus came to the town of Bethany, Mary anointed His head and feet with perfume to prepare Him for His burial because she believed His word. Her faith and love were precious to Jesus. He said that wherever the gospel was preached, what she did would be told in memory of her.[27]

Before Mary anointed Jesus, her brother Lazarus was deathly ill. Mary and Martha called for Jesus to heal him, but He did not come. When Jesus heard of Lazarus's sickness, He said, "This sickness is not to end in death, but for the glory of God, so that the Son of God may be glorified by it" (John 11:4). Yet Lazarus died. Mary and Martha were heartbroken. Four days later, Jesus came. When Jesus saw Mary and all the other Jews weeping, He wept. He asked them to take Him to Lazarus's tomb. He told them to roll away the stone. Martha resisted, but Jesus said, "Did I not say to you that if you believe, you will see the glory of God?" (John 11:40). They rolled away the stone, and Jesus cried out with a loud voice, "Lazarus, come forth!" Lazarus stood up, having been raised from the dead! Jesus told them to unwrap him and restore him to his sisters. Many of the Jews then believed in Him.[28]

Raising a man from the dead was the last straw for the Pharisees. Soon all Israel would follow Jesus! From that day on, the Pharisees plotted to kill Him.[29]

Notes

1 Matthew 8:26–27

2 Matthew 14:13–21

3 John 2:1–11; Luke 5:3–11; Matthew 17:27

4 Matthew 21:18–22; Luke 22:50–51; Mark 5:24–34

5 Matthew 14:26

6 Matthew 11:5

7 Luke 4:33–36

8 Mark 1:25–26

9 Hebrews 2:4

10 John 6:66

11 John 6:26–27

12 Luke 23:21

13 John 6:68–69

14 Matthew 27:18

15 Matthew 21:46

16 Matthew 9:11–12

17 Matthew 22:15–22

18 Matthew 9:36

19 Luke 10:38–42

20 Mark 1:35

21 Luke 6:12

22 John 5:17–18

23 John 5:20–24

24 Matthew 16:21

25 John 12:32

26 Luke 9:22

27 John 12:1–7; Matthew 26:7, 13

28 John 11:1–46

29 John 11:47–53

PART 5

Jesus's Crucifixion

He made Him who knew no sin
to be sin on our behalf,
so that we might become the
righteousness of God in Him.

– 2 Corinthians 5:21

13

The Final Week
Jesus Establishes
the New Covenant

*This cup which is poured out for you
is the new covenant in My blood.*

– Luke 22:20

*J*ews flooded Jerusalem for the Passover. It was lamb selection day. Each family was required to choose a lamb to sacrifice. And God chose His lamb.[1]

He came meekly, riding on a donkey.[2] Crowds threw their garments before Jesus, waving palm branches and crying out, "Hosanna to the Son of David!" (Matthew 21:9). The Pharisees were angry—even the children were praising Him! They said to Him, "Do you hear what these children are saying?" Jesus answered, "Yes; have you never read, 'Out of the mouth of infants and nursing babies You have prepared praise for Yourself'?" (Matthew 21:16). God raised up children to praise His Son as a testimony to the spiritually blinded adults who were looking for a political hero instead of a sin-bearing Savior.

That evening, Jesus and His disciples went to the village of Bethany to visit His friends Lazarus, Mary, and Martha.[3] He lodged there each night of the Passover week while teaching in Jerusalem during the day. At this time, Mary anointed Him with perfume, while Judas looked on in disgust, thinking of all the money he could have had if she had sold the perfume.[4] In fact, Judas kept the money bag for Jesus. Whenever anyone gave Jesus money, Judas held it for Him. Judas frequently stole from the money bag because he was a lover of money.[5] This sin would cause him to bring about his own downfall and eternal condemnation.[6]

As Jesus's suffering and death drew near, He became greatly troubled. But He encouraged Himself, saying, "What shall I say, 'Father, save Me from this hour'? But for this purpose I came. . . . Father, glorify Your name" (John 12:27–28). Not long after that, Judas went to the religious leaders and said, "What are you willing to give me to betray Him to you?" (Matthew 26:15). They weighed out to him thirty pieces of silver. From that moment on, Judas looked for an opportunity to betray the Lord.[7]

On Thursday evening, Jesus sat down with His disciples for the Passover.[8] Rising from the table, He laid aside His garments and wrapped a towel around Himself. He poured water into a basin and began to wash the disciples' feet, wiping them with the towel. He said, "Do you know what I have done to you? . . . If I then, the Lord and the Teacher, washed your feet, you also ought to wash one another's feet. For I gave you an example" (John 13:12–15). Jesus was teaching the disciples to humble themselves by serving and caring for one another.

Then Jesus shocked them all when He said, "Truly, truly, I say to you, that one of you will betray Me" (John 13:21). Cut to the heart, they each said, "Surely not I, Lord?" (Matthew 26:22). Jesus said, "He who dipped his hand with Me in the bowl is the one who will betray Me" (Matthew 26:23). After Jesus dipped and gave the bread to Judas, Satan entered Judas.[9] Jesus said to him, "What you do, do quickly" (John 13:27). Judas went out, and it was night.

While the rest of the disciples reclined at the table, Jesus said, "I have earnestly desired to eat this Passover with you before I suffer" (Luke 22:15). Jesus desired to eat this supper because it was the sign of the covenant He was to make with them through His death on the cross. The supper represented His undying love for His people and the price He was to pay to redeem them from God's wrath and curse. It represented everything He came for, all that He had labored, prepared, and prayed for, and all that the Father had given Him to do—that is, to purchase His people with His blood and make them one with Him, forever.

To initiate the sign of the new covenant, Jesus took bread, broke it, and said, "This is My body which is given for you" (Luke 22:19). The bread was not really His body, but it represented His body, which was to be broken for sinners. Likewise, He took the cup and gave thanks, saying, "This cup which is poured out for you is the new covenant in My blood" (Luke 22:20). The cup represented His blood, which was shed for the forgiveness of sins. While introducing the sign of the new covenant, He gave the terms of the new covenant: "A new commandment I give to you, that you love one another. . . . By this all men will know that you are My disciples" (John 13:34–35).

Then Jesus said, "You will all fall away because of Me this night, for it is written, 'I will strike down the shepherd, and the sheep of the flock shall be scattered.' But after I have been raised, I will go ahead of you to Galilee" (Matthew 26:31–32). Peter said, "Even though all may fall away because of You, I will never fall away" (Matthew 26:33). Jesus said, "Truly I say to you that this very night, before a rooster crows, you will deny Me three times" (Matthew 26:34). Peter said, "Even if I have to die with You, I will not deny You" (Matthew 26:35). All the disciples said the same thing.

Jesus told them not to worry because He was going to the Father for them and would come back to receive them to Himself.[10] He said it was better that He go because He would send the Holy Spirit, who would be with them always.[11] The Holy Spirit would reveal Christ's glory, bring to remembrance His word, and be the means of their communion with the Father and the Son.[12]

Jesus told His disciples that He loved them with the same love the Father had for Him.[13] He encouraged them to abide in His love, for apart from Him, they could do nothing. If they would abide in Him, they would bear much fruit. He warned them that the world would hate them because it hated Him, but the Holy Spirit would comfort them and empower them to witness for Him.[14] These promises were not just for the twelve disciples but for everyone who would follow Him down through the ages.[15]

Jesus said that if they asked anything in His name, He would do it. By answering their prayers, the Father would be glorified in the Son, and their joy would be full.[16] He prayed that the Father would glorify Him that He might glorify the Father by giving eternal life to all whom the Father had given Him. He prayed that His disciples would behold His glory, so their joy in Him would be full. He asked the Father to keep them in His name that they might be one, even as the Father and the Son are one, so the world might believe that the Father had sent Him and loved them. He prayed that the Father would keep them from the evil one and sanctify them in His word.[17] Then He closed their time with a hymn and departed to the garden to pray.[18]

Notes

1. See Ray Vander Laan's That the World May Know video series.
2. Matthew 21:4–8
3. Matthew 21:17
4. Matthew 26:6–13
5. John 12:6
6. Matthew 26:14–15; 1 Timothy 6:9–10
7. Matthew 26:16
8. John 13:1–17
9. John 13:27
10. John 14:1–4
11. John 16:5–7; 14:16–17
12. John 16:13–15, 26
13. John 14:21; 17:23
14. John 15:1–10, 18–27
15. John 17:20
16. John 14:13–14; 16:23–24
17. John 17:1–3, 11, 13, 15–17, 21, 23–24
18. Mark 14:26

14

Thy Will Be Done
Jesus Submits to the Cross

My Father, if this cannot pass away unless
I drink it, Your will be done.

— Matthew 26:42

*A*s Jesus entered the garden, the weight of His
people's sins began to press upon Him. He
said, "My soul is deeply grieved, to the point
of death; remain here and keep watch with Me" (Matthew 26:38). Then He fell on His face and prayed, crying out, "Abba! Father! All things are possible for You; remove this cup from Me; yet not what I will, but what You will" (Mark 14:36).

He came back and found the disciples sleeping. He said, "Could you not keep watch for one hour? Keep watching and praying that you may not come into temptation; the spirit is willing, but the flesh is weak" (Mark 14:37–38). He went a second time and prayed, "My Father, if this cannot pass away unless I drink it, Your will be done" (Matthew 26:42). When He came back, He found His disciples sleeping again. He went a third time and prayed with such agony that large drops of blood burst through His skin.[1] He cried out, "Father, if You are willing, remove this cup from Me; yet not My will, but Yours be done" (Luke 22:42). When He arose, He said to His disciples, "Are you still sleeping and resting? Behold, the hour is at hand and the Son of Man is being betrayed into the hands of sinners" (Matthew 26:45).

While He was still speaking, Judas came with a great multitude carrying swords and clubs. Judas instructed them, "Whomever I kiss, He is the one; seize Him" (Matthew 26:48). Judas kissed Jesus and said, "Hail, Rabbi!" (Matthew 26:49). When the men moved to seize Jesus, Peter took his sword and swung it, cutting off one of their ears. Jesus picked up the ear, put it back on, and said to Peter, "Put the sword into the sheath; the cup which the Father has given Me, shall I not drink it?" (John 18:11). Then the religious leaders took Jesus away, and all His disciples fled.

Peter and John followed at a distance. While Jesus was being questioned, Peter warmed himself by the fire. A servant-girl said, "This man was with [Jesus] too" (Luke 22:56). But Peter denied it, saying, "I do not know Him" (Luke 22:57). Another person said, "You are one of them," but Peter said, "I am not!" (Luke 22:58). A third person reported, "This man was with Jesus!" Then Peter cursed and swore, shouting, "I do not know the man!" (Matthew 26:74). Immediately, a rooster crowed. Jesus caught Peter's eye across the courtyard, and Peter remembered His words, "Before a rooster crows, you will deny Me three times" (Matthew 26:75). Peter went out and wept bitterly.

The high priest asked Jesus, "Are You the Son of God?" Jesus answered, "Yes, I am" (Luke 22:70). Tearing his clothes, the high priest cried out, "Blasphemy!"[2] To blaspheme is to curse God or try to steal His position and authority. According to Jewish law, blasphemers were to be put to death.[3] But Jesus never blasphemed. He is the Son of God! He perfectly loved and obeyed His Father. He lived to glorify His Father by doing His will. Yet, as the sins of His people were put upon Him, God used wicked men as the means to condemn Him for their sin.[4]

The religious leaders delivered Jesus to Pilate to have Him put to death. Pilate asked, "Are You the King of the Jews?" Jesus answered, "It is as you say" (Matthew 27:11). Pilate sent Jesus to Herod. Herod's soldiers put a royal robe and a crown of thorns on Him. They mocked Him, saying, "Hail, King of the Jews!" (Matthew 27:29). Jesus did not resist but subjected Himself to their cruelty, in fulfillment of the Scripture, "He was oppressed and He was afflicted . . . Like a lamb that is led to the slaughter, and like a sheep that is silent before its shearers, so He did not open His mouth" (Isaiah 53:7).

When Herod saw that Jesus would not answer him, he sent Jesus back to Pilate. Pilate knew Jesus was innocent. He declared, "I find no guilt in this man" (Luke 23:4). Since it was the custom to release a prisoner during Passover, Pilate said, "Do you want me to release for you the King of the Jews?" (Mark 15:9). The crowd yelled out, "Away with this man, and release for us Barabbas!" (Luke 23:18). Now, dear children, you must know that Barabbas was a robber and murderer. When Pilate said, "What then shall I do with Jesus?" the people kept crying out, "Crucify, crucify Him!" (Luke 23:21).

In response to their demands, Pilate let a robber and murderer go free but condemned Jesus to death. That was terribly wrong, wasn't it? Jesus was innocent, and Barabbas was guilty. But you know what? We are guilty like Barabbas. We have the sin of robbery and murder in our hearts and worse. Barabbas represents us. We deserve to be condemned. But because of Jesus's death in the place of sinners, those who believe in Him are free from God's judgment, wrath, and curse! It is more shocking for God to free sinners from judgment than for Pilate to free a murderer, because the offense of sin is measured by the worth of the One against whom we have sinned.

In the providence of God, Pilate condemned Jesus to death.[5] While Barabbas was running free, Jesus was being nailed to the cross between two robbers. People yelled, "If you are the Son of God, come down from the cross" (Matthew 27:40). Yet, because He was the Son of God, He stayed on the cross. That is why He came. That is why the Father was pleased with Him—because He laid down His life for sinners.[6] Only the Son of God could bear the Father's wrath for the sins of His people without being destroyed. Only He was qualified to be the sin-bearer because He alone was righteous and of infinite worth. Only He was able to be the sin-bearer because He was both God and man.

Notes

1 Luke 22:44
2 Matthew 26:65
3 Leviticus 24:16
4 2 Corinthians 5:21; Acts 2:23
5 Acts 2:23
6 John 10:17

15

In the Place of Sinners
Jesus's Suffering and Death

God demonstrates His own love toward us,
in that while we were yet sinners,
Christ died for us.

– Romans 5:8

*J*esus was crucified between two robbers. At first, they were both hurling insults at Him, but then one of them rebuked the other, saying, "Do you not even fear God, since you are under the same sentence of condemnation? And we indeed are suffering justly, for we are receiving what we deserve for our deeds; but this man has done nothing wrong" (Luke 23:40–41). Looking at Jesus, he said, "Jesus, remember me when You come in Your kingdom!" (Luke 23:42). Jesus said to him, "Truly I say to you, today you shall be with Me in Paradise" (Luke 23:43). At that very moment, Jesus was paying for the sins of the robber, assuring him that He would accomplish his salvation and secure for him eternal life. The man who lived an entire life of sin was promised forgiveness and heavenly rewards because Christ died in his place!

During His crucifixion, Jesus appeared to most as a mere man. But angels recognized Him as the Son of God. The One whom they had seen high and lifted up, the One whom they served with fear and trembling, had now humbled Himself by becoming obedient to the point of death, even death on a cross.[1] It was shocking enough to see Him leave the throne and take on human flesh, but to lower Himself to the scorn of men, to be made sin on behalf of His people, and to bear the wrath of His Father to save the enemies of God—this was more than their minds could grasp. Every mouth in heaven must have dropped as they beheld the sins of God's people being placed on God's Son. At that moment, the Father declared Him "guilty" and accursed. He turned away from Jesus and released His wrath on Jesus's soul.

When sin was placed on Jesus, darkness permeated all creation—even the sun had no light. Jesus cried out, "My God, My God, why have You forsaken Me?" (Mark 15:34). He was forsaken because He was made sin for His people that they might be forgiven and made right with God.[2] At three o'clock on Friday afternoon, when the horn sounded to let everyone know that the Passover lamb had been slain, Jesus, the true Passover Lamb, cried out with a loud voice, "It is finished!" (John 19:30).[3] He had satisfied the Father's wrath. He finished His work and accomplished **redemption** for His people. Then He exclaimed, "Father, into Your hands I commit My Spirit" (Luke 23:46). With a loud cry, He gave up His spirit and died. When the Roman centurion saw how Jesus breathed His last, he praised God, saying, "Truly this man was the Son of God!" (Mark 15:39). At that moment, the veil in the temple tore from top to bottom, showing that sinners now have free access to the Father through the Son.[4]

What does the suffering and death of Jesus mean? It shows that God publicly displayed His justice through Jesus's blood so He could forgive sinners and reconcile them to Himself.[5]

You might ask, "How can God's wrath against a multitude of sinners be removed by the death of one man?" It is because of the immeasurable worth of the Man. Jesus's blood is of more value than liquid gold because it flows from the God-man who is perfectly righteous and fully divine.[6] There is enough value in His blood to purchase myriads and myriads of souls! The Bible says that Jesus's offering of Himself as a sacrifice in the place of sinners is a fragrant aroma to God.[7] The Father accepted it, being pleased with His Son and all who come to Him through His Son. The debt for their sin has been paid in full. The list of sins that stood against them has been canceled, being nailed to the cross.[8] They are forgiven for every sin committed, being pronounced "Not guilty!" The Father's wrath against them has been satisfied. Justice has been accomplished by the punishment of an infinitely righteous Man in the place of sinners.

Moreover, God credits Jesus's righteousness to those who trust in Him. He looks at them and declares,

"Righteous!" because He sees them in Christ.[9] God made Jesus, who didn't have any sin, to be punished for sin, that they might be made righteous in God's sight. In other words, Jesus took their sin so they could have His righteousness.[10] Why do sinners need Christ's righteousness? Only those who are righteous can have fellowship with God. God did not send His Son to suffer in the place of sinners just so they could be forgiven of sins, freed from the curse of the law, and saved from God's wrath, though those things are so very wonderful! He did it so He could be just in reconciling them to Himself as adopted sons and daughters, lavishing on them all the love and favor He has for His Son![11] He did it so He could bring them into His special presence and shower them with all His Fatherly love, that they might behold and reflect His glory. Only the Son of God dwells in the Father's special presence. Therefore, only those who have the Son's righteousness can join the Son in the Father's presence. This is what Christ purchased for sinners—a dwelling place in the Father's presence! They were bought with a price—the precious blood of Christ—so they could be made one with God forever. The purpose of Christ's death is to make a way for God to be just in having fellowship with sinners. There is no way He can do this unless their sin is paid for and they are credited with Christ's righteousness.

Justice had to be satisfied, sin had to be removed, and perfect righteousness had to be credited for sinners to draw near. God did this for sinners in sending His Son to die in their place. But, dear children, please do not think it was easy for Him. It was costly. It was painful. It was more terrible than words can describe. Creation turned dark that day. God did not spare His Son, His only Son, when sin was placed on Him. God executed His wrath on Him to the fullest extent.[12] This shows how offensive sin is to a holy God. If God did not spare His own Son—the One in whom He was well-pleased—when sin was placed on Him, then He will not spare anyone who does not come to Him through faith in His Son.[13]

To confirm Jesus's death, a Roman soldier thrust a sword into His side, causing water and blood to gush out. Pilate granted Joseph of Arimathea and Nicodemus permission to bury Jesus's body. They wrapped His body in linen cloths and laid it in a new tomb that had been cut out of the rock. Then they rolled a large stone against the entrance of the tomb and went away.[14]

A few of the women watched Jesus's death and burial from a distance. They had wanted to anoint His body, but since the tomb was sealed and the sun had set, they quickly went home. The next day they rested, according to the Sabbath. They planned to return to the tomb early Sunday morning to anoint Him.[15]

The Pharisees remembered that Jesus said He would rise again on the third day, so they asked Pilate to secure the tomb with Roman soldiers who would guard it day and night. Pilate granted their request, and soldiers guarded the tomb.[16]

Notes

1 Philippians 2:8

2 2 Corinthians 5:20–21

3 Matthew 27:45; see Ray Vander Laan, That the World May Know video series.

4 Matthew 27:50–51

5 Romans 3:25; Proverbs 17:15 says, "He who justifies the wicked and he who condemns the righteous, both of them alike are an abomination to the Lord." God's justice requires that He judge sinners. The question, therefore, is how can God be just and justify the sinner? The answer is found in Romans 3:21–26, "But now apart from the Law the righteousness of God has been manifested . . . even the righteousness of God through faith in Jesus Christ for all those who believe; for there is no distinction; for all have sinned and fall short of the glory of God, being justified as a gift by His grace through the redemption which is in Christ Jesus; whom God displayed publicly as a propitiation in His blood through faith. This was to demonstrate His righteousness . . . that He would be just and the justifier of the one who has faith in Jesus." God can be just and justify the sinner because Jesus Christ satisfied the requirements of the law by His righteous life and substitutionary death on the cross in the place of sinners. Paul Washer explains, "On the cross, [Jesus] stood in the place of His guilty people, and their sin was imputed to Him (2 Corinthians 5:21). As the Sin-Bearer, He became accursed of God, forsaken of God, and crushed under the weight of God's wrath (Galatians 3:13; Matthew 27:46; Isaiah 53:10). His death paid the debt for sin, satisfied the demands of God's justice, and appeased His wrath. In this manner, God solved the great dilemma. He has justly punished the sins of His people in the death of His only Son and therefore may freely justify all who place their hope in Him." Paul Washer, The Gospel's Power er and Message (Grand Rapids: Reformation Heritage Books, 2012), 165.

6 This thought comes from Puritan author John Flavel.

7 Ephesians 5:2

8 Colossians 2:14

9 Romans 5:9

10 2 Corinthians 5:21

11 Galatians 3:26; 2 Corinthians 6:16–18; John 17:23

12 Romans 8:32

13 This thought is from John Flavel.

14 John 19:34, 38–42; Matthew 27:60

15 Luke 23:55–56

16 Matthew 27:62–66

PART 6

Jesus's Resurrection, Ascension, and Exaltation

The God of our fathers raised up Jesus. . . .
He is the one whom God exalted to
His right hand as a Prince and a Savior,
to grant repentance . . . and forgiveness of sins.

– Acts 5:30–31

16

Mission Accomplished!
Jesus's Resurrection

> He is not here, for He has risen,
> just as He said.
>
> – *Matthew* 28:6

*O*n Sunday morning, Jesus rose from the dead! He is alive! Death could not hold Him. His resurrection is proof that He is the Son of God and that God accepted His sacrifice as full payment for sin. This is the best news on earth for those who believe. Since Christ paid for their sins, God is just in removing the list of sins against them, having nailed it to the cross.[1]

Imagine the indescribable joy Jesus felt as He was resurrected. He must have come up with a shout of victory! How the angels and seraphim must have exploded with praise. He did it! He saved His people! He purchased their forgiveness with His blood. He defeated sin, death, and Satan. He conquered the cross. He glorified the Father. He is alive!

The resurrection of Jesus Christ proves that He had no sin of His own, since death could not keep Him. He was sinless, so He had to rise! It also proves that He accomplished His Father's will by redeeming a people for Himself. It declares that God is just to forgive sinners and treat them as if they never sinned. He is just to reward them as if they lived a life of perfect obedience. He is just to unite them to Himself, give them His Spirit, and love them with all the love He has for His Son.[2] He is just to declare them righteous in His Son. He is just to allow them to be seated with His Son in heavenly places above all creation—even above angels.[3] He is just to allow them to share His Son's eternal rewards.[4] Best of all, He is just to allow them to partake of the fellowship between the Father and the Son.

After being raised, Jesus neatly folded His grave-clothes and walked through the stone with inexpressible joy.[5] Then an angel removed the stone so everyone could see that He had risen.[6] Several women arrived to anoint His body, thinking He was still dead. When they saw the stone rolled away and the angels standing beside it, they were afraid. The angels said, "Why do you seek the living One among the dead? He is not here, but He has risen. Remember how He spoke to you while He was still in Galilee, saying that the Son of Man must be delivered into the hands of sinful men, and be crucified, and the third day rise again" (Luke 24:5–7). "Go quickly and tell His disciples that He has risen from the dead" (Matthew 28:7). As the women departed from the tomb, Jesus met them on their way. When they saw Him, they took hold of His feet and worshiped Him.[7]

After the women ran to the disciples, Mary Magdalene, who had not yet seen Jesus, walked about the garden tomb, weeping. She looked in and saw two angels sitting where Jesus's body had lain. They said to her, "Woman, why are you weeping?" She said, "Because they have taken away my Lord, and I do not know where they have laid Him" (John 20:13). When she said this, she turned around and saw Jesus, but she did not recognize Him. She thought He was the gardener.

Isn't that strange? The crucified and risen Lord looked like a gardener? Do you have any idea why she did not recognize Him? If you said because He had a glorified body, you are right. He was perfectly healed from all His wounds and any physical imperfections. All that remained were the holes in His hands, feet, and side. These are precious memorials. They speak of the price He paid to redeem His people, and they serve as a sign of the new covenant.

But there might have been another reason Mary Magdalene did not recognize Jesus. Just as before His death no one could recognize Him without the Spirit, so after His resurrection, no one could recognize Him without the Spirit. Seeing Jesus with physical eyes was not enough for salvation, even when He was seen in His glorified body. He still appeared as an ordinary man. The Spirit had to reveal Him as the crucified and risen Son of God.

Jesus asked Mary Magdalene why she was weeping. Still thinking He was the gardener, she said, "Sir, if you have carried Him away, tell me where you have laid Him, and I will take Him away" (John 20:15). Then Jesus said, "Mary!" (John 20:16). Immediately, she recognized Him and worshiped.

Jesus told Mary Magdalene, "Go to My brethren and say to them, 'I ascend to My Father and your Father, My God and your God'" (John 20:17). Mary ran to the disciples, exclaiming, "I have seen the Lord" (John 20:18).

When the women told the disciples that Jesus had risen from the dead, the disciples thought they were crazy.[8] Even the Pharisees remembered that Jesus said He would rise.[9] But His disciples forgot—worse yet, they simply did not believe. Peter and John ran to see the empty tomb, but they still did not understand.[10]

That evening, two disciples walked on the road to Emmaus, talking about the events of the day. Jesus came over and walked beside them, but they were prevented from recognizing Him. Of course, they saw Him, as Mary Magdalene did, but they were blinded to who He was. They thought He was an ordinary man. He asked what they were talking about. They answered, "Are You the only one visiting Jerusalem and unaware of the things which have happened here in these days?" (Luke 24:18). Jesus asked, "What things?" They replied, "The things about Jesus the Nazarene" (Luke 24:19). They explained how they had hoped He would save Israel, but He had been crucified, and now it was the third day since it had happened. They also said that several women claimed He was alive, but when the disciples went to see the tomb, they did not see Him.

Jesus said, "O foolish men and slow of heart to believe in all that the prophets have spoken! Was it not necessary for the Christ to suffer these things and to enter into His glory?" (Luke 24:25–26). Beginning with Moses and the prophets, Jesus explained how all the Scriptures were about Him and His work on the cross to save sinners. When they reached their destination, the disciples invited Jesus to stay for supper. When Jesus took bread and broke it, their eyes were opened to recognize Him. Immediately, He vanished from their sight.[11]

After this, the two ran to tell the other disciples that they had seen Jesus. While they were talking, Jesus appeared and stood among them. The disciples were frightened, thinking they were seeing a spirit. Jesus said, "Why are you troubled, and why do doubts arise in your hearts? See My hands and My feet, that it is I myself; touch Me and see, for a spirit does not have flesh and bones as you see that I have" (Luke 24:38–39). Then Jesus asked for something to eat. They gave Him fish, and He ate in front of them.

Do you think Jesus ate fish because He was hungry? No, Jesus wasn't hungry. He ate to prove that He had a real, resurrected body. After Jesus ate, He said that He had fulfilled all the things written about Him in the Law of Moses, the Prophets, and the Psalms.[12] Then He opened their minds to understand the Scriptures, and they believed.[13]

All the disciples saw Jesus, except for Thomas, who was not there. The disciples told Thomas, "We have seen the Lord!" But Thomas said, "Unless I see in His hands the imprint of the nails, and put my finger into the place of the nails, and put my hand into His side, I will not believe" (John 20:25). Eight days later, the disciples met together, and Thomas was with them. While the doors were closed, Jesus appeared and stood among them, saying, "Peace be with you." He looked at Thomas and said, "Reach here with your finger, and see My hands; and reach here your hand and put it into My side; and do not be unbelieving, but believing" (John 20:27). In an act of worship, Thomas cried out, "My Lord and my God!" (John 20:28). Jesus said to him, "Because you have seen Me, have you believed? Blessed are they who did not see, and yet believed" (John 20:29).

Notes

1 Colossians 2:14

2 Luke 24:46–47; Romans 7:4; Acts 2:33; Ephesians 1:13

3 Ephesians 2:6; 1:21

4 Romans 8:17

5 John 20:6–7

6 Matthew 28:2

7 Matthew 28:8–9

8 Luke 24:11

9 Matthew 27:63

10 John 20:6–10

11 Luke 24:31. See vv. 13–35 for the entire story.

12 Luke 24:44

13 Luke 24:45

17

Witnesses to His Resurrection

Jesus Gives
the Great Commission

You will receive power when the Holy Spirit
has come upon you; and you shall be My
witnesses . . . to the remotest part of the earth.

– Acts 1:8

The resurrection of Jesus Christ is amazing! He was declared the Son of God with power by the resurrection.[1] It was a power so strong that it was magnetic, causing believers who had died before Him to rise from the dead with Him.[2] This testified to His completed work on the cross and **foreshadowed** the resurrection of all believers at the end of the age. Jesus's resurrection was so powerful that even the dead could not remain unaffected![3] The **firstfruits** of His labor were abundant, pointing to an immeasurable harvest of believers from all the nations!

After His resurrection, Jesus walked on the earth for forty days. During that time, He appeared to the women, the eleven disciples, and more than five hundred disciples at once.[4] He also appeared to His earthly brother, James.[5] Before Jesus's resurrection, James mocked Jesus.[6] But Jesus loved James. When Jesus appeared to James after His resurrection, James believed and was counted among the disciples. In fact, James even wrote a letter that is included in the New Testament—the book of James. Jesus's other earthly brothers—Jude, Joseph, and Simon—also came to faith after His resurrection,[7] and Jude's letter is in the New Testament. What a marvelous, glorious Savior!

After Jesus's resurrection, Peter, John, and several others went fishing. At the break of dawn, the men were about to give up since they had fished all night and caught nothing. Then they saw a man on the beach who called out, "Cast the net on the right-hand side of the boat and you will find a catch" (John 21:6). They did as he said, and so many fish swam into their net that they could not lift it into the boat. John shouted, "It is the Lord!" (John 21:7). Peter threw on his clothes, jumped in the water, and swam to Jesus as fast as he could. When the others rowed ashore, they saw that Jesus had prepared breakfast. Jesus told them to bring the fish they had caught. Peter retrieved the fish. Then Jesus said, "Come and have breakfast" (John 21:12). Jesus gave them bread and fish, and He ate with them.

Do you remember when Jesus first called Peter to the ministry? Jesus told Peter to let down his net, and so many fish swam into the net that the boat began to sink. That was when Jesus told Peter he would be a fisher of men. Now, after His resurrection, Jesus told Peter to let down his net, and he caught another boatload of fish. Do you know why Jesus did this a second time? It was to restore Peter to the ministry after Peter had denied Him. Jesus had paid for Peter's sin so Peter could be forgiven. Now Jesus was reinstating Peter as a preacher of the gospel—but first, Jesus gave Peter the opportunity to repent.

Three times Jesus asked Peter, "Do you love Me?" Three times Peter answered, "You know that I love You."[8] Then Jesus said, "Shepherd My sheep."[9] Peter was to show his love for Jesus by caring for His people and teaching them His Word. The time would come for Peter to die for Jesus. But for now, Peter was to fulfill his ministry. Jesus finished Peter's call with the same words He used to begin it three years earlier: "Follow Me!"[10]

After these appearances, Jesus gathered His disciples at Bethany to commission them to be His witnesses. He said, "It is written, that the Christ would suffer and rise again from the dead the third day, and that repentance for forgiveness of sins would be proclaimed in His name to all the nations, beginning from Jerusalem" (Luke 24:46–47). He commanded them to wait in Jerusalem for the promise of the Holy Spirit, who would empower them to be His witnesses. He said, "All authority has been given to Me in heaven and on earth. Go therefore and make disciples of all the nations, baptizing them in the name of the Father and the Son and the Holy Spirit, teaching them to observe all that I commanded you; and lo, I am with you always, even to the end of the age" (Matthew 28:18–20).

While Jesus was saying these things, He was lifted up, and a cloud received Him out of their sight. Then two angels appeared and said, "Men of Galilee, why do you stand looking into the sky? This Jesus, who has been taken up from you into heaven, will come in just the same way as you have watched Him go into heaven" (Acts 1:11). Then the angels disappeared. Angelic appearances were rare. When God wanted to verify a special event, He sent angels to bear witness. Angels were present at Jesus's birth, resurrection, and ascension. They testified that He is God and that these events are the work of God.

The disciples returned to Jerusalem with great joy, praising God and waiting for the promise of the Holy Spirit.[11] They devoted themselves to prayer and continued with one mind, men and women together, including Mary, the mother of Jesus, and His brothers. They were about 120 people in all.[12]

Notes

1 Romans 1:4
2 Matthew 27:52–53
3 Not only were the physically dead affected but, most importantly, the spiritually dead! See Ephesians 2:5.
4 1 Corinthians 15:6
5 1 Corinthians 15:7
6 John 7:5
7 Acts 1:14
8 John 21:15–17
9 John 21:16
10 John 21:19
11 Luke 24:52–53
12 Acts 1:14–15

18

The Ascended King
Jesus's Coronation and Exaltation

> God highly exalted Him, and bestowed on
> Him the name which is above every name.
>
> *– Philippians 2:9*

*D*ear children, where did Jesus go when He went up? If you said into heaven, you are right![1] The disciples last saw Him in the clouds, but the Scriptures give us a glimpse of what happened next.

Jesus ascended into heaven with a shout of victory![2] Heaven's gates unlocked, and its doors swung open as He made His triumphant entry.[3] All heaven cried out, "Who is this King of glory?" (Psalm 24:10). It is the Lord Jesus Christ! He is the King of Glory! Angels bowed down before Him as He proceeded to the throne. But wait—who are those men, women, and children following Him? How did they enter through the gates? How could they ascend to the Holy Place? They are His **spoils** from His victorious death and resurrection—they are His reward! They are His captives who willingly follow

Him wherever He leads, having been made one with Him through His blood.[4] How Satan seethes in defeat, cringing to see them follow Jesus to the throne. Though Satan cannot stop this spectacular procession, he still attempts to keep others from being added to it. He cannot stand to see Christ glorified by this faithful following of souls—but Christ's blood is victorious every time. Souls are continually added to this glorious **train**, to the praise of the Captain of our salvation! The gates of heaven swing open for all who die in Christ, that they might be part of His majestic procession and ascend to the Holy Place, where He is seated in all His glory.[5] Praise God for His amazing grace!

After His triumphant ascension, Jesus took His seat at the Father's right hand, where He was exalted and crowned King of kings.[6] He was given dominion and a people from every nation who would serve Him.[7] His death on the cross was vindicated by His heavenly **exaltation**.[8] He was given the name that is above every name.[9] At the name of Jesus, every knee will bow, of those who are in heaven, on earth, and under the earth, and every tongue will confess that He is Lord.[10] He is King of kings and Lord of lords, and His kingdom will have no end![11]

He is seated above all rule, authority, power, dominion, and every name that is named.[12] All angels are put in subjection to Him.[13] All things are put under His feet. He is given to His people as head over all, and He rules for their good and His Father's glory.[14]

His enemies are defeated by His heavenly exaltation. He disarmed them, making a public display of them by triumphing over them through His death, resurrection, ascension, and exaltation.[15] Satan is crushed, and all that awaits him is certain condemnation.[16] The Man Christ Jesus is exalted, and all that awaits Him is eternal glory—glory that He will share with His people, to the praise of the glory of His Father!

Do you know why Jesus's exaltation is so amazing? It is because He is exalted not only as the Son of God but also as the Man, Christ Jesus. As the Son of God, Jesus left His place of exaltation, humbled Himself by becoming a man, and was obedient to the point of death, even death on the cross.[17] God raised Jesus from the dead and exalted Him in His human body to God's right hand. There, Jesus represents His people and makes **intercession** for them.[18] He who was the highest became the lowest. Because of His humiliation, He is exalted above all, not only as the Son of God but also as a man—as one of us! The fact that He is exalted in His human body forever testifies to the salvation He accomplished for His people. Every time the Father looks at His beloved Son, He sees one of our kind—a human like us!

Dear children, do you know what Jesus did next as the exalted King of kings? He sent the gift of the Holy Spirit. Do you know why the Holy Spirit is a gift? He is a gift because He changes sinners' hearts. He helps them see their sinfulness. He opens their eyes to recognize Jesus as Lord and Savior. He helps them repent of their sins and trust in Jesus. He unites them to the Father and the Son.[19] He helps them pray and understand God's Word.[20] He gives them to the desire to know, love, and obey God.[21] He helps them grow in godliness. He unites them to other Christians.[22] He reminds them of God's love.[23] He comforts them in their suffering. He empowers them to witness for Christ.[24]

What is Jesus doing now as the exalted King of kings? He is reigning over all.[25] He is building His church.[26] He is interceding for His people.[27] He is preparing their rewards.[28]

Notes

1 Acts 1:11
2 Psalm 47:5
3 Psalm 24:7–10
4 Ephesians 4:8
5 2 Timothy 2:12
6 Daniel 7:9; Hebrews 2:7
7 Daniel 7:14
8 Ephesians 4:8
9 Philippians 2:9
10 Philippians 2:10–11
11 Daniel 7:14
12 Ephesians 1:21
13 1 Peter 3:22
14 Ephesians 1:22–23
15 Colossians 2:15; Ephesians 1:21–22
16 Genesis 3:15; Revelation 20:10
17 Philippians 2:8
18 Hebrews 7:25
19 John 14:23
20 John 14:26; Romans 8:26
21 Hebrews 8:10–11
22 Ephesians 2:18; 1 Corinthians 12:13
23 Romans 5:5
24 Acts 1:8
25 Ephesians 1:20–22
26 Matthew 16:18
27 Hebrews 7:25; Daniel 4:17, 35
28 Matthew 10:42; Luke 6:23, 35; Colossians 3:24; Revelation 22:12

PART 7

King Jesus's Call to Sinners

The time is fulfilled, and
the kingdom of God is at hand;
repent and believe in the gospel.

– *Mark 1:15*

19

Bow Before the King
Repent and Believe

Therefore repent and return, so that
your sins may be wiped away.

– Acts 3:19

When Jesus sent the Holy Spirit, He changed the world forever. Now men, women, and children from every tribe, tongue, and nation are being added to His glorious kingdom. It began ten days after Jesus ascended into heaven when 120 of His followers gathered to pray during a Jewish holiday called Pentecost.[1] As they were praying, a noise came from heaven like a rushing wind, and it filled the whole house. Something like tongues of fire rested on each of the men and women as they were filled with the Holy Spirit. They began speaking of the mighty deeds of God in many different languages![2]

When the people in Jerusalem heard this, they wanted to know what was happening. Peter answered them boldly by proclaiming the gospel. He said that

God had shown them that Jesus is the Savior, yet they crucified Him. But on the third day, God raised Him from the dead and seated Him at His right hand, where He received the Holy Spirit to give to His people, as they had witnessed on that day.[3] Therefore, God exalted Jesus as Lord and Savior, and the gift of the Holy Spirit is the proof of His exaltation. The people were cut to the heart and cried out, "Brethren, what shall we do?" (Acts 2:37). Peter, filled with the Holy Spirit, said, "Repent, and each of you be baptized in the name of Jesus Christ for the forgiveness of your sins; and you will receive the gift of the Holy Spirit" (Acts 2:38). Three thousand people repented and were added to the church that day.[4]

Dear children, the same Holy Spirit is calling you to repent and believe in Jesus today. Do you know what it means to repent? The Children's Catechism teaches, "To repent is to be sorry for sin, and to hate it and forsake it, because it is displeasing to God."[5] Repentance is agreeing that we have sinned against God and feeling sorrow for our sin. This sorrow causes us to turn to God and submit to His Word.

Repentance is not a work that saves us. Rather, it is the outward sign of a heart that has been changed to love and obey God. It is not a one-time action—it is a way of life. The person who is truly repentant will *continue* to repent as he or she is made aware of sinful attitudes and actions that displease the Lord. To be repentant does not mean that we never sin, but that when we do sin, we confess it and forsake it. Simply put, to repent is to stop doing the wrong thing (such as stealing or gossiping) and start doing the right thing (such as giving or speaking well of others) because this pleases the Lord. Repentance is the outward proof of a truly believing heart.

Dear children, just as at Pentecost, the Holy Spirit is calling you to repent of your sins and believe in Jesus today. Do you know that you have sinned against God? Will you repent of your sins? Will you trust in Jesus alone for salvation?

Notes

1   Acts 1:15
2   Acts 2:1–4
3   Acts 2:22–24, 32–33
4   Acts 2:41
5   *Catechism for Young Children: An Introduction to the Shorter Catechism*, Question 56.

20

Trust the King
Confess and Believe

Believe in the Lord Jesus,
and you will be saved.

– Acts 16:31

*D*ear children, the King of Kings has summoned you. He calls you to repent of your sins and believe in Him. What does it mean to believe? To believe is to live by faith. Faith is trust in God and His promises. God's promises are in the Bible. What has God promised concerning salvation? The Bible says, "Believe in the Lord Jesus, and you will be saved" (Acts 16:31). Do you believe in Jesus? To believe in Jesus is to trust His righteous life and His death on the cross as the only way to save you from God's wrath and bring you into a right relationship with God. The Bible says, "But to the one who does not work [or try to earn his salvation], but believes in Him who justifies the ungodly, his faith is credited to him as righteousness" (Romans 4:5). To believe is to rely on Christ's work for us, not our own works or obedience. It is to recognize that the only way we can be accepted by God is through Christ's obedience in our place. The Bible also says, "We have believed in Christ Jesus, so that we may be justified [which means to be made right with God] by faith in Christ and not by the works [our own obedience] of the Law" (Galatians 2:16). Are you trusting in your own righteousness and good behavior to be saved, or do you recognize that you are a sinner who has no righteousness of your own? If you recognize that you are a sinner with no righteousness, there is good news for you!

The good news is that Jesus Christ died on the cross to save sinners. To believe in Jesus is to trust His death on the cross as payment for your sins. The Bible says, "Christ also died for sins once for all, the just for the unjust, so that He might bring us to God" (1 Peter 3:18). To believe is to recognize that we have broken God's law. We agree that God would be just to punish us. But by faith we cling to the promise that God will forgive us because Christ paid the penalty for our sin. We confess our sins and trust in the blood of Jesus to cover us. We rest in this promise: "If we confess our sins, He is faithful and righteous to forgive us our sins and to cleanse us from all unrighteousness" (1 John 1:9). We not only confess our sins, but we also forsake them. The Bible says, "He who conceals [or covers] his transgressions [or sins] will not prosper, but he who confesses and forsakes them will find compassion" (Proverbs 28:13).

It is important to know that believing in Jesus is not a one-time decision—it is a life-time commitment. The person who truly believes in Jesus for salvation will *continue* to believe Him and His promises for this life and the life to come. This is what it means to live by faith. The Bible says the righteous shall live by faith. Faith is to believe God's Word. We prove that we believe God's Word by doing what it says. We do what it says not to *become* saved but because we *are* saved and want to follow Him. This is the proof that we truly believe.

Dear children, Christ Jesus came into the world to save sinners.[1] Are you a sinner? Then Christ's death is for you! Confess your sins and trust Him to forgive you and cleanse you from all unrighteousness. Rely on Jesus's righteous life and death on the cross to make you right with God. Run from your sins into the arms of the Savior. Believe in the Lord Jesus, and you will be saved!

Notes

1   1 Timothy 1:15

21

Kiss the King
Judgment Is Coming

Kiss the Son, lest he be angry,
and you perish in the way,
for his wrath is quickly kindled.
Blessed are all who take refuge in him.

— Psalm 2:12 (ESV)

*J*esus will come back as King of kings and Lord of lords.[1] He will take His seat as Judge.[2] He will judge the living and the dead according to His Word.[3] He will appoint everyone to eternal punishment for every sin they have committed.[4] Only those who have repented of their sins and trusted in Christ will be saved from judgment and enter eternal life with Him in the new heavens and the new earth.[5]

What a good and gracious God to warn us of coming judgment and to provide a way of escape through His Son! That reminds me of the life of Noah. Do you remember how God told Noah He was going to judge the world with a flood because of people's sin? If that were all God said, Noah would have perished with the rest of the world. But God graciously made a way of escape. God told Noah to build an ark, giving him the exact dimensions so the ark would not be destroyed by the flood. By faith, Noah obeyed God and built the ark just as God had said. Then Noah called men, women, and children to come into the ark to be saved from God's judgment.[6] Other than Noah's family, no one came. No one believed that God would send a flood. No one believed that God would punish them for their sins.

We struggle with that same unbelief today. We don't really believe God will punish us for our sins because it has not happened—yet. But it will happen. Just as the flood came and everyone outside the ark drowned, so we will all stand before the judgment seat of God to receive just payment for our sins. But there is hope. Even as God provided a way of escape for Noah, so He has provided a way of escape for us. Jesus is our way of escape—He is the ark of our salvation. He is the way to be saved from God's wrath and reconciled to Him. But we must repent and believe in Jesus, or we will not be saved. In the days of Noah, it was not enough for people to hear about the ark. It was not enough for people to believe the ark existed. They had to actually go into the ark, by faith, to be saved. In the same way, it is not enough to know about Jesus. It is not enough to believe that Jesus exists. We must repent of our sins and trust in Him to be saved.

Do you remember when we talked about the wise man and the foolish man in the introduction? The wise man is the one who hears God's Word and acts on it.

The foolish man is the one who hears God's Word but does not act on it. You know what happened to the foolish man when the storms came. Dear children, I hope you are not like the foolish man. I hope you are like the wise man who hears God's Word and acts on it. Now is the time to act on God's Word. Today is the day to repent of your sins and trust in Christ alone to be made right with God. He is your only refuge—He is your only salvation!

Notes

1   Revelation 19:15-16
2   John 5:22; Acts 17:31
3   2 Timothy 4:1; Acts 10:42; John 12:48; Romans 2:16
4   Matthew 25:46; Romans 2:5-6
5   John 3:15-16; 2 Peter 3:13
6   2 Peter 2:5

PART 8

Evidence of a Right Relationship with the King

"I will dwell in them and walk among them;
And I will be their God,
and they shall be My people.
Therefore, come out from their midst and be
separate," says the Lord. . . .
"And I will be a father to you,
And you shall be sons and daughters to Me,"
Says the Lord Almighty.

– *2 Corinthians 6:16–18*

22

New Heart
A Changed Relationship
with God

I will give you a new heart and
put a new spirit within you. . . .
I will put My Spirit within you and
cause you to walk in My statutes . . .
so you will be My people,
and I will be your God.

– Ezekiel 36:26–28

D ear children, do you wonder if you truly believe in Christ? It is a very important question,
and I hope you are thinking about it. There is
nothing more important than having a right relationship with God through faith in Jesus Christ. The Bible
tells us we can know if we believe because those who
believe have a changing life.[1] No one can be made right
with God and remain unchanged.

That makes me think of a story I once heard.[2] A
visiting preacher showed up an hour late for church.
When he got up to preach, he apologized for being

late. He explained that he had a flat tire, and when he got out of his car to change it, he was run over by a semitruck. Now, children, you must know, this man had a neatly pressed suit, well-combed hair, and not a single scratch on his body. What do you think? Was he telling the truth? Do you believe that he was run over by a semitruck? You might say, "No, that man is lying!" I think you are right. But what if I told you that he was really sincere—that he really believed he had been run over by a semitruck? Then you might say, "That man is crazy!" And you are right. He would be crazy! That man did not get run over by a semitruck. How do we know? We know because if he had, he would have been changed. He most likely would not be alive, and if he had survived, he would have been in the hospital for a very long time. He certainly would not be preaching at the church an hour later.

Dear children, do you know that it is just as **illogical** for a person to say he has had an encounter with the living God and remain unchanged? A person who has been made right with God through faith in Jesus Christ will have a changing life that is becoming more like Christ.[3] The first evidence of belief is that he is trusting in Christ's death on the cross for forgiveness of sins and Christ's righteous life for acceptance with God.[4] He has **renounced** all self-righteousness, confessing that he has no righteousness of his own. He agrees that God would be just to punish him for his sins, yet by faith, he clings to Christ's offer of salvation. He places all his hope in Christ for a right relationship with God.

His relationship with God is changed from unbelief, **hostility**, and rebellion to faith, love, and growing obedience.[5]

The Bible also says that the one who truly believes in Christ has fellowship with the Father and the Son.[6] This means that he delights in spending time with God in His Word and in prayer. Before, he had no desire to be with God, but now he looks forward to spending time with God. Before, he might have read the Bible to please his parents, or maybe he did not read the Bible at all, but now he reads the Bible because he wants to. His soul is nurtured and strengthened by spending time with God. Like a newborn baby, he longs for the pure milk of the Word.[7] He agrees with the psalmist who says, "I delight in Your law" (Psalm 119:70). He has been given a new heart that loves and obeys God. He wants to keep God's commandments and walk in His ways.[8] God's commandments used to be like a heavy chain around his neck, but now they are his delight.[9] He knows that he believes because he keeps God's commands.[10]

He also delights to be in God's presence through prayer. He used to find prayer boring, but now he wants to bring his requests to God and pray for others. As he prays, he sees a pattern of answered prayer.[11] This does not mean that every prayer is answered immediately or as expected, but he has confidence that God hears him.[12] He witnesses God's gracious intervention in his life in a way that can only be explained by answered prayer. He is learning to depend on God in prayer for everything, and he not only finds himself praying longer but many times throughout the day.[13] He cannot explain this new desire except that it is a work of God's Spirit in him.[14]

His primary desire is to love the Lord his God with all his heart, soul, mind, and strength.[15] Jesus Christ is his greatest treasure. He counts all things as loss compared to the surpassing value of knowing Him.[16] He can say with the psalmist that the steadfast love of the Lord is better than life![17] No one has to say to him, "Know the Lord," because knowing Christ is what he wants to do.[18] In fact, he is even ready to suffer loss for the sake of Christ. His love for Christ is such that his love for others—even those he loves most—looks like hate in comparison.[19] If he has to choose between those he loves most and following Christ, he will choose to follow Christ—even if it costs him his life. He knows that by losing his life, he will gain it.[20] He will suffer some degree of persecution for the sake of Christ, and though it might pain him, he will not deny his Lord.[21]

He would rather suffer than sin against God.[22] He used to want to be in control of his life, but now he submits to the decree, will, and authority of his heavenly Father, trusting that He knows best and is working all things together for his good.[23] He begins to recognize God's fatherly discipline in his life, knowing that discipline is a sign of belonging to God, since God disciplines every son and daughter He receives.[24] This discipline is not just for "big sins" but is the lifelong process God uses to chip away everything in the believer that is not like Christ.[25] While the discipline is painful for the moment, the believer learns to trust his heavenly Father through it.[26] He begins to think of trials with joy because they are opportunities to prove that his faith is real.[27] He rests in the promise that his suffering will seem short and easy compared to the eternal weight of glory God is preparing for him.[28] He learns to look not at the things that are seen, but at the things that are not seen.[29] He recognizes that this earth is not his home, but his **citizenship** is with Christ in heaven.[30] He sets his mind on the things above, where Christ is, and not on the things of this earth.[31] Then he can truly say, "For to me, to live is Christ and to die is gain" (Philippians 1:21).

His growing desire is to glorify God, and his true hope is that Christ will be honored in his body, whether by life or by death.[32] He used to live to make everyone think he was great, but now he lives to show that God alone is great! His great joy is to be used by God to manifest His beauty and display His worth as it is revealed in the gospel. He recognizes that he was bought with a price, so he wants to glorify God with his body.[33] His deepest sorrow is when he dishonors God by his sin.

Notes

1 The book of 1 John was written so we might know that we have eternal life (1 John 5:13). The following chapters in this book are written to provide evidence of saving faith so children might have a biblical assurance of salvation.

2 This thought is from Paul Washer.

3 Romans 8:29

4 For the sake of simplicity, generic masculine pronouns are used to describe the evidence of a true believer, both male and female.

5 Romans 5:1–2, 10–11; 8:28, 31, 37–39

6 1 John 1:3–7

7 1 Peter 2:2

8 Ezekiel 36:26–28

9 1 John 5:3

10 1 John 2:3. This does not mean that he never disobeys God's commands but that the general pattern of his life is one of growing obedience and a desire to please God.

11 1 John 3:21–22

12 1 John 5:14–15

13 John 15:7; 1 Thessalonians 5:17

14 While there may be times that he doesn't feel God's presence or struggles with apathy, his general disposition toward God has been changed from enmity to love so that even during dry seasons, trials, and spiritually low points, his faith remains.

15 Luke 10:27

16 Philippians 3:8

17 Psalm 63:3

18 Jeremiah 31:34

19 Luke 14:26

20 Matthew 10:37–38; Matthew 16:25

21 Mark 10:30; 2 Thessalonians 1:4; Romans 8:17; 2 Corinthians 1:5; Philippians 1:29; 2 Timothy 3:12; Matthew 10:32–33

22 Hebrews 11:25; 1 Peter 3:17

23 Romans 8:28

24 Paul Washer, The Gospel Call and True Conversion (Grand Rapids: Reformation Heritage Books, 2013), 112; Hebrews 12:5–12.

25 Romans 8:29

26 Hebrews 12:11; James 1:2–3

27 1 Peter 1:7

28 2 Corinthians 4:17

29 2 Corinthians 4:18; 1 John 3:1–3

30 Philippians 3:20

31 Colossians 3:1–2

32 Philippians 1:19–20

33 1 Corinthians 6:20

23

New Life
A Changed Relationship
with Sin

> Our old self was crucified with Him, in
> order that our body of sin might be done
> away with, so that we would no longer
> be slaves to sin. . . . Even so consider
> yourselves to be dead to sin, but alive to
> God in Christ Jesus.
>
> – *Romans* 6:6, 11

*D*ear children, have you ever seen an apple tree? How did you know it was an apple tree? You knew it was an apple tree because it had apples on it! Similarly, we can know if a person believes in Jesus by looking at the fruit of his life.[1] By "fruit" we mean a person's thoughts, desires, and actions. Are they pleasing to God? Are they becoming more like Jesus? Are they growing in obedience to His Word? Someone who has been united to God by faith in Jesus Christ will bear good fruit, proving to be His disciple.[2] Some will bear more fruit than others,[3] but all will bear good fruit that lasts to eternity.

The person who believes in Jesus will bear good fruit because he has become a new person in Christ.[4] He has been rescued from the power of sin and made a member of Christ's glorious kingdom. He is no longer a slave to sin.[5] Through Christ's death, he has been made dead to sin, and through Christ's resurrection, he has been made alive to righteousness.[6] This does not mean that he never sins. It means that when he does sin, he has a godly sorrow leading to repentance.[7] The sin he once loved, he now hates.[8] He confesses his sin to God and trusts in the blood of Jesus Christ to cleanse him. He turns from his sin and uses the means God has given him to resist it, such as the Bible, prayer, corporate worship, and fellowship with believers. He takes the necessary steps to make things right with those he has wronged and seeks to live in peace with all people.[9]

Even if he falls seven times, he always gets up again.[10] He will not give up the fight.[11] He is learning to put sin to death through prayer and the sword of the Spirit, which is the Word of God.[12] He used to battle against God, but now he battles against his sin. He recognizes that sin is his greatest enemy because it threatens his fellowship with God. His love for God is such that he would rather have fellowship with God than enjoy the pleasures of sin.[13] This is the evidence that he is being led by the Spirit of God. Those who are led by the Spirit of God are children of God.[14] They have received a spirit of adoption by which they cry out, "Abba! Father!"[15] The Holy Spirit bears witness with their spirits that they are children of God.[16]

The person who believes in Christ has put to death his sinful desires.[17] His life is marked by the Spirit.[18] He shows the fruit of love, joy, peace, patience, kindness, goodness, faithfulness, gentleness, and self-control.[19] This does not mean that he never stumbles or sins, but the overall pattern of his life is growing in the grace and knowledge of the Lord Jesus Christ.[20] He is becoming more like Jesus each day.[21] A new Christian is not going to be as mature as an older Christian, yet he will have a genuine desire for godliness. Sometimes it is an uphill battle, with three steps forward and two steps back.[22] Yet by God's grace, the believer stays the course, keeping his eyes on the prize God has prepared for him in Christ.[23]

The entire nature of the believer's life has been transformed. His thoughts and desires have been changed by Scripture, so he no longer wants to live like the world.[24] He recognizes that friendship with the world makes him God's enemy.[25] He does not love the world or anything in it, for the Bible says if anyone loves the world, the love of the Father is not in him.[26] More and more, he feels like a traveler passing through this world because his real home is with Christ in heaven. For this reason, he is not storing up for himself treasures on earth. Rather, he is storing his treasures in heaven by giving his time, energy, and money to the spread of the gospel. In fact, he used to hold tightly to his earthly possessions, but now he freely gives because in Christ he has freely received.[27]

Notes

1   Matthew 7:20

2   John 15:8

3   Matthew 13:8

4   2 Corinthians 5:17

5   Romans 6:17

6   Romans 6:6, 19, 22

7   2 Corinthians 7:10

8   This thought is from Paul Washer.

9   Matthew 5:23–24; Romans 12:18

10   Proverbs 24:16

11   1 Timothy 6:12

12   Romans 8:13; Ephesians 6:17–18

13   Hebrews 11:25

14   Romans 8:13–14

15   Romans 8:15

16   Romans 8:16

17   Galatians 5:24

18   Romans 8:4–9; 1 John 3:24; 4:13

19   Galatians 5:22–23

20   2 Peter 3:18

21   Romans 8:29

22   Paul Washer, *The Gospel Call and True Conversion*, 112.

23   Philippians 3:14

24   Romans 12:2

25   James 4:4

26   1 John 2:15

27   Matthew 10:8

24

New Mission
A Changed Relationship
with Others

By this all men will know that you are My
disciples, if you have love for one another.

— John 13:35

One of the most remarkable changes in those
who believe is the love they have for other believers.[1] They almost instantly become aware
of their union with others in Christ.[2] Regardless of
ethnicity, age, background, social status, or color, they
share a common bond in Christ that the world cannot
understand. Jesus said, "By this all men will know that
you are My disciples, if you have love for one another"
(John 13:35). This love causes them to treat other believers with kindness and to sacrifice for them.[3] They
willingly give themselves and their belongings to one
another.[4] They show their love for Christ by their love
for one another.[5] This proves that they belong to Him
and is the supernatural result of being born again.[6] In

fact, no one can love God and hate his brother or sister in Christ.[7] Faith in Christ and love for other Christians are inseparable.[8] We know that we truly believe because we love our brothers and sisters in Christ.[9] This love is a work God does in His people's hearts. It is evidence that they belong to Him.

As a result of this love, the one who truly believes in Christ wants to be with Christ's people. He desires to join them in giving praise to God through corporate worship.[10] He loves the church because it is established by God and purchased with Christ's blood. [11] While he recognizes that the church is made up of sinners saved by grace, just like him, he loves them because they belong to Christ. The church is where his love, patience, and humility are often tested, stretched, and forged. He becomes more like Christ, not because it is easy to love other believers but because sometimes it is very hard. Yet, for the sake of Jesus, he does not give up.[12] It is only by continuing to love other believers, even when it is painful, that he proves his faith is real.[13]

The Bible says that true believers have fellowship with one another.[14] When we hear the word "fellowship," we often think of cookies and punch or picnics and luncheons. While gathering to eat can provide a special time to share what God is doing in our lives, this is not the primary meaning of fellowship. Fellowship is more about laboring together to spread the gospel and less about eating food. It suggests a wartime mentality that recognizes we are in a spiritual battle.[15] We must work together to continue in the faith and take the gospel of Jesus Christ to all the peoples of the world.[16] In fact, the apostle Paul urged believers to strive *together* for the faith of the gospel.[17]

Jesus Christ commissioned the church to take the gospel to all nations, and those who belong to Him want to join this mission.[18] Often, when a person comes to believe in Jesus, the first thing he wants to do is tell others about Him.[19] He cannot help but speak of the great things God has done for him![20] He wants everyone to know Christ and be saved from their sins. He starts to feel **burdened** for the lost and wants to work with others to spread the knowledge of Christ in every place.[21] He begins to love even the most unlovable person because he is filled with the love of God in Christ. He learns to bless when he is cursed, do good to those who hate him, and love his enemies.[22] He remembers that when he was an enemy of God, Christ died for him.[23]

The believer longs to be used by God to bring as many people to faith in Christ as possible.[24] He desires to present them to the Lord as his reward.[25] If he is not called by God to preach, he fervently prays for and supports those who are, recognizing this as his part in fulfilling the Great Commission.[26] He begins to grasp something of the meaning of eternity and longs to live in light of it.[27] He wants to live so that at the time of his death it may be said, "Well done, good and faithful servant. . . . Enter into the joy of your master" (Matthew 25:23 ESV). He recognizes that he must give an account to God and lives his life accordingly.[28] Whether he lives or dies, it is all for the Lord.[29]

Even the youngest believer will see some of the above fruit in his life.[30] It might not be as much as the mature believer, but that does not mean it is not genuine.[31] Those who truly believe in Jesus are walking the same narrow way.[32] Others may be farther down the path, but they are all going in the same direction, and they all have the same desire—to love and glorify the Lord Jesus Christ.[33]

The Bible says we are to examine ourselves to see if we are in the faith.[34] Dear children, it is time to examine yourselves. Do you believe in Jesus? Have you repented of your sins? Is there evidence of saving faith in your life, such as love for Christ, keeping His commandments, battling sin, walking in the Spirit, love for the church, concern for the lost, and commitment to do your part in taking the gospel to all nations? Are you living in light of eternity as one who must give an account to God?[35]

If you do not see any of the above fruit in your life, now is the favorable time—today is the day of salvation.[36] Seek the Lord while He may be found; call on Him while He is near.[37] He promises that He will save all who come to Him.[38] Will you repent of your sins and trust in Christ to be made right with God? If so, call out to Him in prayer, asking Him to forgive you, to save you, and to make you a new person in Christ.

Notes

1 1 John 4:12

2 1 Corinthians 12:12–14, 26–27; Ephesians 2:22

3 John 13:34

4 1 John 3:17; 2 Corinthians 8:3; Philippians 2:29–30; Romans 16:4

5 Matthew 25:40

6 1 Peter 1:22–23; 1 John 4:7

7 1 John 4:20

8 Ephesians 1:15; Colossians 1:4; 1 Thessalonians 3:6; 2 Thessalonians 1:3; Philemon 1:5; Hebrews 6:10; 1 John 3:23

9 1 John 3:14

10 Acts 2:46–47

11 Ephesians 2:19–22

12 John 15:12–14; 1 John 5:2

13 Don Currin. Used with permission.

14 1 John 1:3, 7

15 David Mathis, "Learning to Fly in the Fellowship," Desiring God, March 12, 2014, http://www.desiringgod.org/blog/posts/learn-to-fly-in-the-fellowship; 2 Timothy 1:8; 2:2–4.

16 Hebrews 10:23–25; 2 Thessalonians 1:3–4; Matthew 28:18–20; Colossians 1:3–8

17 Philippians 1:27

18 Matthew 28:18–20; Philippians 1:3–7

19 Mark 5:19–20

20 Psalm 66:16; 71:15–16

21 2 Corinthians 2:14–16; 2 Thessalonians 1:8–10

22 Matthew 5:44; 1 Corinthians 4:12; 1 Peter 2:12

23 Romans 5:8–11

24 1 Corinthians 10:33

25 1 Corinthians 3:11–14

26 Philippians 1:27

27 2 Corinthians 4:18

28 Romans 14:12; 1 Peter 1:17–19

29 Romans 14:7–8

30 Matthew 7:16–20

31 Matthew 13:8

32 Matthew 7:14

33 Ephesians 6:23–24

34 2 Corinthians 13:5

35 Romans 14:12

36 2 Corinthians 6:2

37 Isaiah 55:6

38 John 6:37

Conclusion

Summary of the Person
and Work of Christ

Jesus Christ is the Son of God, who took a human body and became a man. He retained all His deity while becoming fully human. For this reason, He is called the God-man. He was born of the Virgin Mary in Bethlehem. His earthly father was Joseph. He grew up in Nazareth. He began His messianic ministry at age thirty. He went all around Israel teaching in the synagogues, preaching the gospel, and healing people. He is the fulfillment of all the promises and prophecies God made in the Old Testament. He is the long-awaited Messiah, the Seed of the woman, the promise to Abraham, and the Son of David. He lived a perfect, sinless life. He kept all the commandments of God and loved Him with all His heart, soul, mind, and strength. He came to earth to do the will of His Father, which is to glorify Him by saving sinners.

Though He had no sin of His own, He was put to death on the cross by wicked men under the rule of Pontius Pilate. There, God punished Him in the place of sinners. After three hours on the cross, darkness fell over the land. By the sixth hour, He gave up His spirit and died, declaring, "It is finished!" He was buried in the tomb of Joseph of Arimathea. On the third day, He arose! Two angels stood by His empty tomb and told the women, "You are looking for Jesus who was crucified. He is not here, for He has risen, just as He said. Tell His disciples that He has risen from the dead!" God showed that He accepted Jesus's sacrifice in the place of sinners by raising Him from the dead.

After His resurrection, He appeared to over five hundred people. He walked on the earth for forty days and ascended into heaven, where He is seated at the Father's right hand, making intercession for His people. He sent down the Holy Spirit to regenerate, sanctify, and seal sinners. Because of His suffering and death in the place of sinners, God exalted Him and gave Him the name that is above every name so that at the name of Jesus every knee shall bow and every tongue confess that He is Lord.

Now God is calling men everywhere to repent of their sins and trust in Jesus's righteous life and sacrificial death for forgiveness of sins, salvation from God's wrath, and acceptance with God. God promises to be the Father of those who come to Him through faith in Jesus Christ and to love them with the same love He has for His Son. Jesus will come back to the earth a second time to gather His people to Himself and judge those who do not love and obey Him.

If the Lord has used this book in your life, please let us at Free Grace Press know.

Also, please visit our website to find the companion study guide to this book as well as other Christian materials that will help you grow in your faith.

Appendix
I Have Just Repented and Believed in Christ. Now What?

If you have just repented of your sins and believed in Christ, we praise the Lord for His grace in you! As a new person in Christ, it is important to develop a regular habit of spending time with God in His Word and in prayer so you can grow in your faith. The Gospel of John is a great place to begin. Read a chapter or two a day. Before you read, ask the Lord to help you understand His Word. You might want to write down what you learn. Then respond to the Lord in prayer, praising Him and thanking Him. When you pray, ask Him to help you see your sins and confess them to Him. Pray for help to live in a way that pleases Him. Bring your needs and requests to Him, and trust Him to take care of you.

It is also important to join a Bible preaching church so that you can be under the care of pastors and have fellowship with believers. If your parents already go to church, cheerfully attend with them, and be an encouragement to others. Listen carefully to the Word as it is being preached, pray that the Lord will help you apply it to your life, and worship the Lord together with those who love Him.

If your parents do not go to church, pray that the Lord would open their hearts, and at the right time, ask if they will take you. If they are willing to take you, ask if a godly older person can disciple you in the faith. Surround yourself with as many godly people as you can. As you grow in Christ, it is important to be a good witness to your parents. One of the main ways you can do this is by honoring them with your kind and respectful behavior.

If your parents are believers, it is just as important to honor and obey them so they can see the fruit of a changed life in you. Show them that you want to learn from them and listen to their instruction so you will grow into a godly person. They are God's gift to you, to teach you and disciple you in the faith.

Be sure to tell others about the good things God has done for you in Christ, and pray for the salvation of unsaved friends and family members. Ask your pastors how you can serve and be a blessing to the church. Pray that the gospel will be preached and believed in all the world.

Finally, make sure to examine everything you hear by God's Word. Let His Word be your standard and your guide. Determine to live for Him no matter the cost. Do everything you can to resist sin and temptation. Pray for strength to be faithful in good and hard times, and keep your eyes on Christ and knowing Him. Whether you eat or drink or whatever you do, do all to the glory of God (1 Corinthians 10:31).

Glossary

burdened – to feel concern for

citizenship – rights, privileges, and duties of belonging to a specific place or people

commissioned – to be sent on a mission

comprehension – the ability to know or understand

conceive – to become pregnant

condescension – to step down in position or honor

confess – to acknowledge

consumed – to take over every part of a person's being

covenant – a binding relationship based on a promise

deity – being God

descendants – children, grandchildren, great-grandchildren, etc.

disposition – thoughts, emotions, and desires

enmity – to be an enemy of

exaltation – to go up in position and honor

exalted – to be honored before and above all others

finite – limited in abilities and qualities

first-fruits – the first ripe fruit of the crop; the first part of something more to come

foreshadow – a small glimpse of something that will happen in the future

hostility – to be against others

illogical – does not make sense

incarnation – to take a human body

insurrection – to rebel against civil government

intercession – to pray to God for another

irreconcilable – unwilling to be friends

just – righteous

justify – to declare righteous

magi – wise men who served the king

manifest – to show or reveal

Messiah – the Savior whom God promised to send

mystery – something hidden or unknown

offering – a sacrifice offered to God as an act of worship

Passover – a special day to remember how God delivered Israel through the blood of a lamb

prophecy – Scriptures that predict Christ's coming

reconcile – to restore peace, favor, and friendship between two people

redemption – to pay the punishment for sin so that sinners can belong to God

render – to give

renounce – to give up

repent – to stop doing the wrong thing and start doing the right thing

saints – people who believe in Jesus

salvation – rescue from sin and judgment; the gift of eternal life with God

spoils – the enemy's treasures that become the victor's reward

stature – reaching a level of physical or intellectual development

synagogue – a Jewish place of worship

testified – to affirm as true

train – a line of people traveling together; a multitude of people following the Lord

treason – to side with the enemy against one's own people

trespass – going the wrong way; sin

vindicate – to restore one's honor by proving his just cause or innocence

zeal – wholehearted devotion

Other Books by Jennifer Adams

A Basket of Summer Fruit, Susannah Spurgeon; edited and annotated by Jennifer Adams

In Love with Christ: The Narrative of Sarah Edwards, Sarah Edwards; edited and annotated by Jennifer Adams

Ann Judson: Missionary Wife, Arabella Stuart; edited and annotated by Jennifer Adams

Delighting in Her Heavenly Bridegroom: The Memoirs of Harriet Newell, Teenage Missionary Wife; edited and annotated by Jennifer Adams

Following Her Beloved: The Memoirs of Henrietta Shuck, Missionary Wife and Mother, compiled by Jeremiah Jeter; edited and expanded by Jennifer Adams

With Cords of Love: The Memoirs of Elizabeth Dwight, Missionary Wife and Mother, compiled by Harrison Dwight; edited and expanded by Jennifer Adams

Jennifer Adams is wife to Scott and mother to four lovely daughters. She has a Master of Arts in Religion from Liberty Baptist Theological Seminary with a concentration in New Testament Greek and is currently a student at Westminster Theological Seminary.

CPSIA information can be obtained
at www.ICGtesting.com
Printed in the USA
BVHW021114210722
642688BV00006BA/430

9 781952 599392